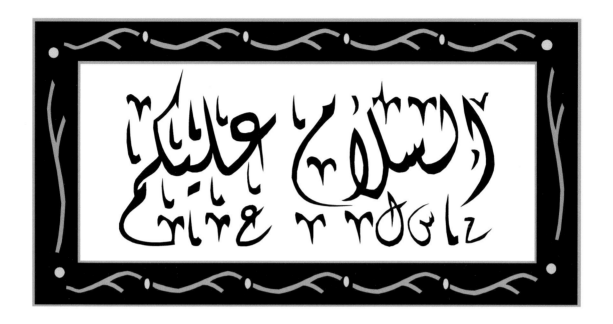

الـعَربية

Alarabia: A Communicative Approach to Learning Arabic for Non-Native Speakers

Mahmoud Amer, Ph.D.

West Chester University of Pennsylvania

D1377700

© 2011 All Rights Reserved

Mahmoud Amer

No part of this publication may be reproduced in any form without the written consent of the author.

For questions and/or inquires, write to

Dr. Mahmoud Amer- Alarabia
Main Hall, S. High Street
Department of Languages and Cultures
West Chester University
West Chester, PA 19383
United States of America

Clip Art images in this document are used under license as defined in the End-User license agreement available in Microsoft Word and also available from Microsoft
http://office.microsoft.com/en-us/tou.aspx#MaterialsthatMicrosoftLicensesToYou

Microsoft Word is a trademark of Microsoft Corporation. All trademarks mentioned in this document are property of their respective owners. Names of characters and places in the conversations provided in this document are fictitious. Any similarity to living people is purely coincidental.

ISBN: 978-0-557-57612-8

Preface: Audience for This Book

This textbook is intended for students who are beginning to learn Arabic at the college level. The lessons in this book are equivalent to two semesters of Arabic language study. Lessons 1 through 7 can be substituted for ARBC 101, and lessons from 8-14 for ARBC 102.

Lessons in this book aim to strike a balance between learning about the language (the structure of Arabic language) and learning the language itself to be able to communicate with native speakers of Arabic using Modern Standard Arabic. This balance allows students to understand how language elements work together to convey meaning, and provide them with an opportunity to practice these functions themselves.

This book provides several ways for students to grab a hold of Arabic by
1. Providing language that students can use in daily conversations
2. Explaining grammatical rules that help learners become better users of language to convey meaning
3. Using authentic language learning material that is spoken by native speakers
4. Using illustrations and images to facilitate learning of new vocabulary
5. Using games to make language learning fun
6. Presenting dialogues that allow students to participate in risk-free class discussions
7. Providing sections reviews, and links functions of interest to students' learning
8. Listing new vocabulary in each section with roots and meaning.
9. Sharing with students experiences of past learners of Arabic through short posts describing strategies and skills learners employed in the past to help them learn.
10. Providing tidbits of information about language functions and their culture relevance.
11. Highlighting cultural and literary connections that might spark students' interest in the language and the culture as well.

Previous editions of this book have been taught over four semesters, and students have been generally pleased with the format and structure of the book. Color schemes that highlight the purpose of each section are provided to help learners navigate the book so easily. The most common theme, however, has been students' interest in the course. Learning Arabic, just like any other language, can be challenging. But it is most certainly fun, and worth the time. There is no better opportunity to learn Arabic than now. It is a language spoken by over 300 million native speakers and official in 22 countries covering two continents. From a cost-benefit analysis, an understanding of Arabic can give you an immediate edge in an ever global and competitive market. Yet, you can never put a price tag on how rewarding your experiences would be when you are able to add 300 million native speakers to your audience, people that otherwise one would not have been able to communicate with, or understand. In other words, the benefits of being able to communicate with people from other cultures are priceless.

Good luck with learning Arabic! I hope you have a fun experience learning Arabic, and I wish you the best in using and learning from this book.

Mahmoud Amer, Ph.D.

Table of Contents

Grammar Topics Covered in This Book

Arabic on Windows and Mac

If you plan on using Arabic on your computer, you might want to think about some of the limitations of using Arabic on a computer.

Notes for Windows Users

In Windows XP, you need to specifically enable Arabic script if you plan on typing in Arabic. Go to *Start/Control Panel/Regional and Language Options*. Choose the *Languages* Tab, and check "the install files for complex script and right-to-left languages (including Thai)" box. After that, hit *apply*. Depending on your computer original configuration, you may be prompted to insert the original XP CD to install these files. When all is done, restart your computer so that new effects take place. Open *Word* or any word-processing software, and press simultaneously the *Shift* then *Alt* buttons. This will change the cursor orientation for Arabic typing. Run a test by typing stuff in Arabic.

Arabic on a MAC

Arabic support is also available for Mac users. Go to *system preferences*, and choose *international*. Follow the steps to install Arabic support. Mac OS provides a variety of layouts for typing in Arabic. Check the documentation of your system for more information.

Arabic on an iPhone/iPod/iPad

If you have an iPhone/iPod, you can also type in Arabic by installing the available Arabic layout on your device. To do this, tap on the *Settings* icon, then select *General/Keyboard*, and then select the Arabic keyboard layout. When you are done, tap in a text field area and select the *globe* icon on the virtual keyboard to switch your language into Arabic.

Arabic on Android Devices

Arabic is available officially on Android devices running Honeycomb 3.0 (the latest Android platform for Android tablets). Arabic support for other Android devices is available via workarounds that involve what's referred to in the community as 'rooting' the device, which voids the warranty on the device. For more information on Arabic on Android devices, visit http://www.ardoid.com/

Alphabet Basics

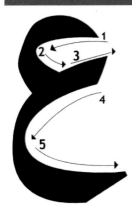

If you have been introduced to the Arabic alphabet before, this unit should be a breeze for you. If this is your first time reading Arabic alphabet, I suggest that you review the exercises available at the end of the book, and use the ones available on the CD (purchased separately). Arabic is fun, and by the end of this course, you will have learned plenty of Arabic to get you started! Arabic is a right-to-left language. This means that when you examine the table below, you should note that the alphabet starts from the right side. In the table below, note that I only provided the English sound equivalent when available. Some Arabic sounds do not have equivalent sounds to them in English. This means that you may not necessarily realize them, but you will be able to in due time. Think of it as a muscle that you have not exercised in a long time. Rest assured that you will be able to recognize them and produce them as well.

Rules for Connecting the Letters

Writing in Arabic is cursive, which means that letters have to be connected together to make words. However, some letters do not follow this rule, and prefer to stand on their own. The ones with the red background¬ in the table above do not follow this rule. To write words in Arabic, there are two main rules that make writing words in Arabic easy. First, to connect a letter to the next one, you will have to chop off the tail, for the most part, of the first letter to connect it to the next. Example:

$$ ب + ا + ب = باب $$

Note that the letters 'و', 'ا', and 'د' do not connect to the next letter, because they belong the family that do not connect to the letters after them. These are in Table 1.

Letters in initial, middle, and end positions

The table below lists all the letters in the Arabic alphabet and their shapes in all possible positions.

Table 1

End	Middle	Initial	Letter	End	Middle	Initial	Letter
ـض	ـضـ	ضـ	ض	ـا	X	ا	ا
ـط	ـطـ	طـ	ط	ـب	ـبـ	بـ	ب
ـظ	ـظـ	ظـ	ظ	ـت	ـتـ	تـ	ت
ـع	ـعـ	عـ	ع	ـث	ـثـ	ثـ	ث
ـغ	ـغـ	غـ	غ	ـج	ـجـ	جـ	ج
ـف	ـفـ	فـ	ف	ـح	ـحـ	حـ	ح
ـق	ـقـ	قـ	ق	ـخ	ـخـ	خـ	خ
ـك	ـكـ	كـ	ك	ـد	X	د	د
ـل	ـلـ	لـ	ل	ـذ	X	ذ	ذ
ـم	ـمـ	مـ	م	ـر	X	ر	ر
ـن	ـنـ	نـ	ن	ـز	X	ز	ز
ـه	ـهـ	هـ	ه	ـس	ـسـ	سـ	س
ـو	X	و	و	ـش	ـشـ	شـ	ش
ـي	ـيـ	يـ	ي	ـص	ـصـ	صـ	ص

Blog

"Learning how to write the Arabic alphabet was very interesting." K

"This week was kind of a culture shock. I never really thought I would be trying to learn the Arabic language. When I saw it on the list of available classes I became excited at the opportunity. I believe learning Arabic would open many doors depending on the paths I may choose for work." J

Letter Shapes

Table 2 lists the main letter shapes in the Arabic alphabet and how they're written out. Note that only base shapes are presented below. For example, if you know how to write ب, you should be able to write ت, and ث since they have the same base shape.

Table 2

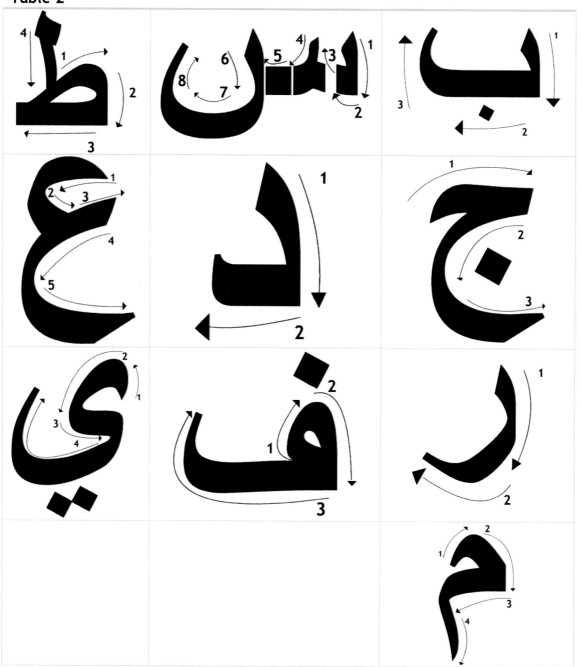

Sounds

Most of the sounds in Arabic exist in the English language. This means that you will not have any trouble pronouncing roughly 70% of the sounds in Arabic. Table 3 lists the Arabic alphabet with letters corresponding to sounds that exist in English.

Table 3

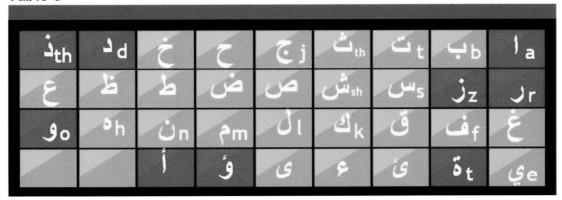

Vowels

Vowels in Arabic can be classified in two main categories: Long vowels, and they are represented by the letters (و ,ا, and ي), and short vowels, which are represented by diacritics called harakat in Arabic (´ and .) as in Table 4.

Table 4

Vowel-short	Vowel-long
´	ا
ُ	و
ِ	ي

The example below shows how these vowels change the pronunciation of other sounds in Arabic. The word being used is من which could mean either *from* or *who* depends on the accent mark being used

1. مَن أحـمد؟ (Sounds close to *men* in English)

2. مِن أحـمد (sounds close to *min* in English)

In addition to these marks, there are other *harakat* that are used in Arabic and that you will see in this book. These are the shadda which looks like this mark ّ and the sukoon which looks like this mark ْ . The *shadda* is used for geminating a sound, sort of doubling it. The *sukoon* is used to clear the consonant of any vowels sounds.

1. عَمّان (Amman)

Connecting the letters

Connect the letters to make meaningful words.

	أ ن ا
	م ن

	أ هـ ل ا ً
	أن تِ
	أي نَ
	تَ ش رّف ن ا

BINGO

Your teacher will give you a bingo table. Every time your teacher says a letter, you need to mark it off on the table. Don't forget to say a BINGO when you have a bingo!

Table 5

ح	ج	ث	ت	ب	أ
س	ز	ر	ذ	د	خ
ظ	ط	ض	ص	س	ش ع
ل	ك	ق	ف	غ	ع
	ي	و	ه	ن	م

Table 6

ل	ك	ق	ف	غ	ع
ح	ج	ث	ت	ب	أ
س	ز	ر	ذ	د	خ
ظ	ط	ض	ص	س	ش م
	ي	و	ه	ن	م

Table 7

	ي	و	ه	ن	م أ
ح	ج	ث	ت	ب	أ
س	ز	ر	ذ	د	خ
ظ	ط	ض	ص	س	ش ع
ل	ك	ق	ف	غ	ع

Numbers

Numbers in Arabic are very easy to learn. Once you learn the numbers from 0-10, you should be well on your way to learning all of them.

خَمْسَة	أَرْبَعَة	ثلاثة	إثْنَان	واحِد
5	4	3	2	1
عَشَرَة	تِسعة	ثَمانية	سَبعة	سِتة
10	9	8	7	6

Stories: The first few classes

In this book, I share with you some of the thoughts of my students as they learned Arabic. These quotes are meant to help you realize the challenges faced by learners in certain aspects of learning a language in general, and Arabic in particular. My students and I hope that these entries help you realize the challenges and rewards that come with learning a language. In addition, the students will be sharing with you tips and skills that they did to help them learn things better in Arabic.

"This week, at the beginning of my elementary Arabic class, I became more excited about Arabic than I was. My one international friend from Yemen taught me a few things and I cannot wait to learn more. I think it is really interesting and fun to learn. Learning about the Arabic alphabet this week was a little confusing, but I am determined to keep practicing and improving. I already know about half of the letters, so I will keep working on the rest. " CD

Literary/Cultural Connection

In this section, I introduce you to phrases, proverbs, or short poems that illustrate features of Arabic culture that might be relevant to each lesson. Examine the saying below:

أهلاً وَ سَهلاً

This saying is used to welcome guests and people to the house. Arabs use this saying liberally when inviting people over, and when trying to make sure guests feel comfortable at their house. It translates to "Welcome home!", meaning *feel free to act, do, and live as you would in your own house.*

Where in the World is this?

This image is of Wadi Rum, also known as وادي القَمَر and it is located about 60 kilometers northeast of Aqaba, Jordan. It is the largest valley in Jordan, and is considered a UNESCO heritage site. For more information about this beautiful place, visit http://www.wadirum.jo/

تَعَارُف Greetings

In this lesson, you will learn how to greet others in Arabic. Some of the expressions used in this lesson are informal, and will be marked with an asterisk * at the list of words at the end of the book (Appendix 1). Please be aware that these expressions are used in specific contexts. When practicing your Arabic, be aware of the context of how the expression is used. If in doubt, ask or email me.

The conversation below illustrates the use of greetings between Arabic native speakers. Samir meets Nadia for the first time, and the conversation below takes place. This dialogue is set in a learning institution. This dialogue however, is applicable in a variety of settings.

المُـفـرَدات Vocabulary

أنا	مِن	أهلاً	أنتِ	أنتَ	أينَ	وَ	تَـشـرّفنـا
I(Am)	From	Welcome	You (Female)	You (Male)	Where	And	Nice To Meet You

شُكراً	عَفواً	مَرحباً	مَساءً	صَباحاً	لَيلاً
Thank You	You're Welcome	Hi/Hello/Welcome	In The Evening	In The Morning	At Night

Colloquial vs. Standard

Note that in standard Arabic, the word 'أينَ' is used instead of the word 'وين'. The latter is used mainly as a colloquial form. Nevertheless, it is often used more than the standard form since the majority of speakers use the everyday colloquial dialect.

مَرحَبـا. أنـا سـامِـر.

Hi! I'm Samir.

				ء	ة	ى	ي	و	هـ	نـ	مـ	لـ	كـ		
						yes		when	hence	neck	met	lent	can		

12 العَربية

أهلاً سامِر. أنا نادية.

Hi Samir! I'm Nadia.

مِن أينَ أنتِ يا نادية؟

Where are you from Nadia?

أنا مِن عَمَّان. و أنتَ مِن أين؟

I'm from Amman. And you?

أنا مِن كلارين

I'm from Clarion.

تَشَرَّفنا

Nice to meet you!

Practice the dialogue with a classmate (if available), so you can feel comfortable pronouncing the words and phrases.

Question Devices: What? ما /ماذا؟

ماذا is used to ask about things, events, and can also be used to ask about the object of the sentence. Example:

subject	verb	What	object	subject	verb
يَقرأُ الطالِبُ؟	يَقرأُ الطالِبُ	ماذا	الكِتابَ.	الطالِبُ	يَقرأُ

What do you wear?

Practice asking questions using ماذا to ask about what your classmates wear to school, work, a night out, and other events.

ملابِس السَهرة	بِنطال	قَميص قَصير الكُمَين	قَميص

فُستان	تَنّورة	حِذاء	جَوارب
لِباس رَسمي	لِباس النوم	شِب شِب	جينز

مـاذا تَـلبَـسُ/ تَـلبَـسـين إلى الجامِعـة؟

Q: What do you wear to school?

ألبَـسُ قَـميصاً و بِـنطالاً!

A: I wear a shirt and pants!

Pronoun Usage

In standard Arabic, there are specific pronouns to address a group of females, or a group of males. Unlike English, where the pronoun you is used to refer a group of both males and females, in standard Arabic, there are pronouns specifically for that. However, most people in informal situations use the pronoun إنتو which can be used to address a group of both males and females.

Pronunciation ع vs. أ

Arabic has sounds that native speakers of other languages may not be familiar with, like the pronunciation of the sound ع which can be easily confused with the sound أ. To help you identify which one is being pronounced, your instructor will pronounce both of them in minimal pairs to help you identify which one is being used. Put a check mark next to the word you hear.

A	أ	ع	B
A	أين	عَين	B
A	أمـر	عَمـر	B
A	ألَـم	عَلَـم	B
A	أسى	عَسـى	B
A	وأدَ	وَعَـدَ	B

The Noun Phrase

Unlike English, Arabic sentences can have a complete thought without using a verb. Examine:

1.   I am a student

2.   أنا طالِـبٌ

Note that sentence (2) is made up of two parts, a pronoun أنا and a noun طالِـب. There is no verb, but the sentence is complete. In addition, note that the gender of the speaker can change the conjugation of the noun. In English, we say *I am a student* or *you are a student* regardless of the gender of the speaker. In Arabic, however, the speaker's gender does matter as far as the pronoun and the noun are concerned. Examine:

3. أنا طالِبٌ (I am a student-male)

4. أنا طالِبةٌ (I am a student-female)

Note the use of ة to mark the gender difference in 4.

Possessive Pronouns (my)

Possessive pronouns in Arabic are very similar to the ones in English. In English, to create a possessive pronoun, you add one of the possessive pronouns before the noun, i.e., *my book, his car, their dog* etc. In Arabic, possessive pronouns are added after the noun as in كِتـابي, which are the word *book* كِتـاب and the possessive pronoun marker ي. If the word ends with a ة, it should be changed into a ت and then the possessive marker ي should be added.

Conjugating the ة and ي

When you add the possessive marker my (ي) to a word ending in ة , the ة must be changed to a regular ت or ت before the marker is added as in the following example:

$$سَيَّارة + ي = سَيَّارَتي$$

Modified Noun in Sentence	Possessive Suffixed added to noun	Possessive Suffix	Noun
أبـي هُوَ مـايك(My father is Mike)	أبـي (my father)	ي	أب (father

Possessive Pronoun (my)

Modify the following nouns by adding the possessive pronoun marker ي and reading the words out loud. Then complete the phrase with information about yourself!

بَلَد	سَيَّارة	هاتِف	شَقّة	إبن	أخ	أب

جامِعة	بَيت	مَدينة	صَديق	حَبيب	أخت	أم

Fill out your ID

If you happen to be in the Middle East, chances are that you may end up filling out some form of some sort. Although most forms are written in both Arabic and English, it might be helpful if you can at least identify the basic common fields, such as your name, address, profession, residence, and signature. Fill out the card below with your information. By the way, the information you enter here is up to you!

Verb Roots

Verb roots are very important in Arabic. They are the basis for complex linguistic classification in the language. In addition, they are used to derive nouns, adjectives, and other parts of speech. Compare

1   كَتَبَ

The root above which means "to write" is called a tri-verb root. Note that the verb is made up of three letters, ك, ت, and ب. In Arabic, certain suffixes and prefixes are used to derive more words from this root. Thus, you should expect any word in Arabic that has to do with writing to contain, in addition to other things, these three letters. For example, the word writer in 2

2   كَاتِب

The word in sentence 2 means "writer." Note that an ا was added after the first letter and the diacritic in the second root letter was changed to ِ .

3   كِتَاب

The word in sentence 3 means "book." Note that an ا was added after the second root letter and the diacritic in the first root letter was also changed.

4   مَكتوب

The word in sentence 4 means "written." Note that an م was added at the beginning of the root, and the letter و before the last root letter.

Derivations

Modify the following words to create derivations based on what you learned in the previous section. Derive the agent based on the example in sentence 2, and the participle based on the example in sentence 4.

participle	agent	root	participle	agent	root
		صَنَعَ	مَعمول	عامِل	عَمِلَ
		زَرَعَ			سَكَنَ
		حَمَدَ			مَنَعَ

The Present Tense: First Person Pronoun

Just like English, the present tense in Arabic is used to refer to events that happen in the present (habitual actions, i.e., I live in the US, I go to work every day at 7, etc). Unlike English, where the verb in the present has one of two states (with third person s, i.e., she works at Subway, or we watch football together), the present tense in Arabic uses suffixes and prefixes depending on the subject of the sentence. Consider the tri-root verb (عَمِلَ) meaning to work. This is the infinitive form (the verb without any suffixes or prefixes). When the agent of the verb is the first person singular pronoun (أنا), an أ is added to the beginning of the verb (sentence 1 below)

1. أنــا أعمَــل في مِكدانــلز (I work at McDonalds).

In certain cases, the pronunciation of the verb changes when it's conjugated.

Conjugate the Verb

Correct the verb in the parentheses to agree with the subject in the following sentences.

1. أنــا (سَكَن) _____ في بَنــسِــلفانــيا .
2. أنــا (حَبَّ) _____ أن أشــاهِدَ بـرنامَج "بونز" .
3. أنــا (ذَهَّب) _____ إلى المَدرَسة .
4. أنــا (نَظَّفَ) _____ البَيت .
5. أنــا (لَعِبَ) _____ كُرة السلّة .

الكِتــابة Writing

Fill out this information card by writing basic sentences about yourself. You can start like this: Hi! My name is Samir. I am from Clarion. I love to watch Family Man.

Hello! مَرحَــبا!

Spelling

Determine the basic shape of the highlighted letter in the following examples. The first two have been completed for you as an example.

	رحَّبَ		حَبَّ	م	جَمَعَ
	صَدَقَ		سارَ	ع	زَرَعَ
	عَمِلَ		شَرَّف		سَمَّى
	مَنَعَ		طَلَبَ		صَنَعَ
	شَهِدَ		كَتَبَ		أقامَ

~	ٔ	ؤ	ٍ	ٌ	ُ	ٕ	~	ء	ة	ى	ي	و	ه	ن	م	ل	ك
						yes	when	hence	neck	met	lent	can

17 العَربية

	نَظَّفَ		لَعِبَ		هَتَفَ
	سَمِعَ		سَكَنَ		وَقَّعَ

Prefixes and Suffixes in Arabic أحْرُف الزِّيادة

To help you remember the prefixes and suffixes in Arabic that are used for several functions, they are grouped into one word which is

Roots

Determine which tri-root the following set of words belong to

meaning	root							
		مَلعَب	مَلعوب		لاعِب		يَلعَب	
		سمَّاعة	مَسموع		سامِع		يَسمَع	
		كِتابة	مَكتوب		كاتِب		يَكتُب	
		قِراءة	مَقروء		قارِئ		يَقرأ	
		جُلوس	مَجلِس		جالِس		يَجلِس	
		مُشاهَدة	شاهِد		مُشاهِد		يُشاهِد	

Identify the Numbers

Write down the words that correspond to the numbers in the following table. The faded lines are provided to help you write neatly!

6   1

7   2

8   3

9   4

10   5

Word Reference

This section lists all roots of the words introduced in this unit and their meaning. Make sure that you are familiar with the meaning of all these roots.

Meaning	Root	Meaning	Root	Meaning	Root
To welcome (welcomed)	رحَّبَ	To love (loved)	حَبَّ	To collect (collected)	جَمَعَ
To be sincere (told the truth)	صَدَقَ	To walk/march (walked/marched)	سارَ	To plant (planted)	زَرَعَ
To work (worked)	عَمِلَ	To honor (honored)	شَرَّفَ	To name (named)	سَمَّى
To prevent (prevented)	مَنَعَ	To request (requested)	طَلَبَ	To make (made)	صَنَعَ
To promise (promised)	وَعَدَ	To write (wrote)	كَتَبَ	To establish/live (established/lived)	أقامَ
To clean (cleaned)	نَظَّفَ	To infanticise (infanticised)	وأدَ	To shout (shouted)	هَتَفَ
To hear (heard)	سَمِعَ	To live (lived)	سَكَنَ	To sign (signed)	وَقَّعَ
To see (saw)	شَهِدَ	To play (played)	لَعِبَ	To go (went)	ذَهَبَ
		To read (read)	قَرَأَ		

Blog

"This was very exciting I love the fact that I can learn little things like this and go back home and teach my family. What we do since there so interested in learning Arabic is we study the words on flash cards first, and we love playing games, so then we used them same flash cards to play Taboo. I don't know if you have ever heard of it but you have this words you have to describe to your teammate what the word is but you can't use a few certain words and them words would be listed on the card under the main word. So for example, if you had the word City, you wouldn't be able to say like town, place, and buildings and maybe like to other words. It's a pretty fun game that me and my family really enjoy and a good learning process." DR

"This week I believe that I have started to' think in Arabic." Some Arabic words get stuck in my head, and when I say something in English sometimes the Arabic equivalent comes to mind. It is more second nature when I start to read, but I am still slow. I feel that after the ordering food lesson, starting to learn the bank information lesson comes so much faster. The more I learn the faster I learn. My lessons in class along with my tutoring sessions have helped critique my understanding of proper word pronunciation and grammar, and motivation through great teaching from people who are passionate about teaching a foreign language, in turn makes me passionate." RV

"This week, we learned how to add the possessive pronoun, *my*, to Arabic words. I think it is pretty easy to remember, but I think I need to be more familiar with the nouns before I actually use the pronoun in sentences. The bingo game we played was a fun attempt to help recognize the letters and sounds. Another game we could play is if we pick a card from a pile of cards with letters on them, and we say what sound that letter makes, and later on we can write words that start with that letter. For the key words we learned, I know the words in Arabic but I just need a little more practice with most of the words with knowing what the words mean because it takes me awhile to remember." CD

Literary/Cultural Connection

In this section, I introduce you to phrases, proverbs, or short poems that illustrate features of Arabic culture that might be relevant to each lesson. Examine the saying below:

البَيتُ بَيتُكَ

This saying is used to welcome guests and people to the house. Arabs use this saying liberally when inviting people over, and when trying to make sure guests feel comfortable at their house. It translates to "The house is yours", meaning *feel free to act, do, and live as you would in your own house.*

Dictation

Write down the words that you hear from your teacher.

Where in the World is this?

This is one of the most recognized places on earth. The Egyptian Pyramids, built thousands of years ago, still stand tall in this magnificent aerial shot. The Pyramids are a proud member of the world wonders and one of the most popular tourist sites in the world. Talk about it if you have visited this place.

هَل تَتَكَلَّم العَربية؟ Do You Speak Arabic?

In this lesson, you will learn how to ask *Yes-No* questions and negate sentences. In addition, you will be introduced to reference nouns in Arabic.

Did you know?

One of the characteristics that define the Arab world is the fact that Arabic is the official and most widely used language in the Arab World! Did you also know that Arabic is one of six official languages of the United Nations? Did you also know it is the 5th most spoken language in the world?

Vocabulary   المُفرَدات

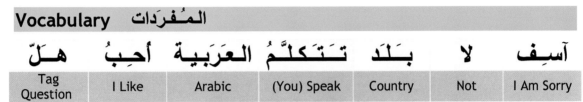

هَلّ	أَحِبُ	العَربية	تَتَكلَّمُ	بَلَد	لا	آسِف
Tag Question	I Like	Arabic	(You) Speak	Country	Not	I Am Sorry

آسِف! أنــا لا أتَكلَّمُ العَرَبية !

Sorry! I do not speak Arabic

مَرحباً! هَل تَتَكلَّمُ العَرَبِية؟

Hi! Do you speak Arabic?

Yes-No Questions

Arabic and English are similar in the sense that speakers of both languages utilize suprasegmentals, intonation and pitch in conversation. Think of the tone you use when you ask a question. Linguistically speaking, a question can be identified structurally and phonetically. In English, when asking a question, you apply inversion, putting the verb before the subject Examine:

You are a student.

Are you a student? (Note the inversion of the subject and verb)

In addition to the inversion, your tone differs in the two previous sentences. When asking a question, you apply rising intonation towards the end of the question.

To create a *yes/no* question in MSA, you add the word هَلْ to the beginning of the sentence. Example: To create a *yes/no* question from the following sentence, you simply add هَلْ to the beginning of the sentence.

أحمَد مِن كلاريــن

هَلّ أحمَد مِن كلاريــن؟

Form Yes/No Questions

Create a yes/no question from the following sentences:

يَـعـمـلُ أحمَد في مَدرَسـة البَنين _____	1
تَـكـتـبُ حنـان في جَريدة الأهرام _____	2
تَدرُسُ حَنـان في جَامِعة كـامبرج _____	3
يَـسـمَعُ نـادِر لِـلموسيقى الكلاسيكية _____	4

Negation النَّفي

Speakers of colloquial Arabic use a variety of ways to negate a sentence. This is because the negating device is dependent on the dialect of Arabic in question. For example, the sentence *I don't want chicken* can be أنا مِش عايز فِراخ in Egyptian ما بِدي جاج in Levantine Arabic, and Arabic respectively. Notice the use of ما and مِش. To simply say *no*, you can use the word لا which means *No!* Examine:

أنـا مِن كلاريــن (I'm from Clarion)

أنـا مِش من كلاريــن (I'm not from Clarion -Levantine dialect)

أنـا مُش من كلاريــن (I'm not from Clarion -Egyptian dialect)

In standard Arabic, a different method is used to form the negative form of the sentence:

أنـا لَسـتُ مِن كلاريــن

Negation

Answer the following questions by saying NO and then negating the sentence:

هَل أنتَ /أنتِ مِن الأردن؟ أنـا مِن الأردن / أنـا لَـستُ مِن الأردن	1
هَل أنتَ/أنتِ طَـبيبٌ؟ _____	2
هَل أنتَ/أنتِ مايكِل/ سانـدرا؟ _____	3
هَل أنتَ/أنتِ على ما يُـرام؟ _____	4

Identity

To play this game, the teacher will assign you several famous people that the whole class is familiar with (Brad Pitt, U2's Bono, Hillary Clinton, etc). The teacher will choose one student to take on the identity of that celebrity. After that, the students start asking yes/no questions to uncover the identity of that person. Whoever identifies the celebrity first wins. The following adjectives are provided to help you! You can also ask your teacher, or tutor to provide more adjectives than the ones below.

مُذيع Broadcaster		مَكروه Despised		سِياسي politician		مُطرب Singer	غَني rich
كَبير Old		عازف composer		لاعِب Player		مُحامي Lawyer	أنثى female
صَغير young		مُمَثّل actor		مَحبوب Popular		مُبَرمِج Programmer	ذَكَر male

Yes/No Questions-Identity Game

To find out the identity of the person, ask questions as in the ones below based on the characteristics defined above. Possible figures: Brad Pitt, Barack Obama, Toni Morrison, Martin Luther King, Bono, the Beatles, Steve Jobs, Bill Gates, Dan Marino, Ben Roethlisberger, Yo Yo Ma.

هَلّ أنـتَ مُطرب؟ لا!
هَلّ أنـتَ مُمَثّل؟نَعم!
هَلّ أنـتَ ذَكَر؟نَعم !
ماذا تُمَثّل؟ أمَثّل دور "تـروي!"
هَلّ انتَ براد بيت؟ نَعَم!

Pronunciation هـ vs. ح

The pronunciation of the sound ح can be easily confused with the sound هـ. To help you identify which one is being pronounced, your instructor will pronounce both of them in minimal pairs to help you identify which one is being used. Put a check mark next to the word you hear.

A	هـ	ح	B
A	هَمزة	حَمزة	B
A	يَهوى	يحوى	B
A	ساهِل	ساحِل	B
A	هَرَم	حَرَم	B
A	هامِد	حامِد	B
A	يُهبِط	يُحبِط	B

This and That: أسـماء الإشارة: هذا و هَذِه

Reference nouns in Arabic can be used to refer to masculine and feminine nouns. هذا is used to refer to masculine nouns and هَذِه is used to refer to feminine nouns. Examples:

هَذِهِ فَتَاةٌ!   هَذا كِتَابٌ!

  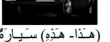   

(هَـذا- هَذِه) دَرّاجَة   (هَـذا- هَذِه)كُرسيٌ   (هَـذا- هَذِه) سَيارةٌ   (هَـذا- هَذِه) مُعَلّمة

(هَـذا- هَـذِهِ) زُجاجة   (هَـذا- هَـذِهِ) فِـنجانٌ   (هَـذا- هَـذِهِ) شَمـسٌ   (هَـذا- هَـذِهِ) قَـمَرٌ

Numbers Review

Cardinal numbers! Would you like to share your birthday with the class?

كانون الأول
December

الثَّاني عشر

تِشرين الثَّاني   **كانون الثَّاني**
November   January

الحَادي عَشر   الأول

تِشرين الأول   **شبـاط**
October   February

العَاشِر   الثَّاني

أيلول   **آذار**
September   March

التَّاسِع   الثَّالِث

آب   **نيسان**
August   April

الثَّامِن   الرَّابِع

تَمّوز   **أيّـار**
July   May

السَّابِع   الخَامِس

العِشرون
الثلاثون   **حُزيـران**
                      June

السَّادِس

عيـدُ ميلادي هُـوَ التـاسِعُ مِن شَـهرِ آذارِ لِعـامِ 1976

Birthday Song

The following song is traditionally sung on someone's birthday (in Egyptian Colloquial Arabic)

سَـنَـة حِـلوة يا جَـميل سَـنَـة حِـلوة يا جَـميل
سَـنَـة حِـلوة يا _____ سَـنَـة حِـلوة يا جَـميل

Question Device: Where أيـنَ

The question device أيـن is used to inquire about the place or location of an event, place, and other relevant information. Consider the example below

يَـذهَـبُ أحمـدُ إلى السـوقِ كُلَّ يـوم.

أيـنَ يَـذهَـبُ أحمـدُ كُلَّ يـوم؟ إلى السـوقِ!

People of the World

Practice asking and answering where these people are from. Guess if you are not sure!

Matt Damon	Gandhi	King Hussein	Fairouz	Bruce Lee
أمـريكـا	الـهـنـد	الأردُن	لُبنـان	الصيـن

Q: مِن أيـنَ مـات دَمِن؟
Where is Matt Damon from?

A: مـات دَامِـن من أمريكـا!
Matt Damon is from America!

Spelling

Find the missing letters in the following words (these are the Key Words items from this unit)

آ ـ فِ ـ بَ ـ د لا لا تَـتَـ لَّمُ الـ رَبَـ ة أ ـ بُ ـ لَّ

Word Reference

This section lists all roots of the words introduced in this unit and their meaning. Make sure that you are familiar with the meaning of all these roots.

Meaning	Root	meaning	Root	Meaning	Root
To program (programmed)	بَـرمَـجَ	To be feminine (became feminine)	أنِـثَ	To be sorry (was sorry)	آسِـف
To defend (defended)	حَمِـيَ	To be in vain (was in vain)	حَـبِـطَ	To love (loved)	حَـبَّ
To broadcast (broadcasted)	ذِيعَ	To study (studied)	دَرَسَ	To contain (contained)	حَـوَى
To become small (became small)	صَغِـرَ	To listen (listened)	سَمِـعَ	To lead (led)	ساسَ
To play (played)	عَزَفَ	To Arabise (Arabised)	عَرَبَ	To compose (composed)	طَرِبَ
To become large (became large)	كَـبِـرَ	To become rich/became rich	غَنِي	To make (made)	عَـمِـلَ
To use words (used words); to speak (spoke)	كَـلِـمَ	To hate (hated)	كَرِهَ	To write (wrote)	كَتَـبَ
To fall (fell)	هَـبَـطَ	To be like (was like)	مَـثُـلَ	To play (played)	لَـعِـبَ
				To long (longed)	هـوَى

Writing الكِـتـابة

Fill out this information card by writing basic sentences about yourself. You can continue adding more information about yourself from things that you have already learned! You can include information about what languages you speak, what you study, and where you study. You can write about your hobbies and things you like to do! It is really about YOU and up to YOU!

Hello!   مَرحَـبـا!

At The Restaurant في المَطعَم

In this lesson, you will learn how to order food at a restaurant using Arabic. In addition, you'll learn how the definite article is used and pronounced in Arabic.

Did you know?

Middle Eastern cuisine is pretty rich and diverse! Food is as important in Arab culture as it is elsewhere. Cooking and eating food is an activity that brings families together, and creates lifetime bonds.

Vocabulary المُفرَدات

دَجاج	لَحمَة	كوب	شَراب	عَصير	كاس	سَمَحتَ لَو
Chicken	Meat	Cup	Beverage	Juice	Glass	If You Please

لَيمون	بُرتُقال	سَلَطة	شوربة	أرُزّ	مَقلي	مَشوي
Lemon	Orange	Salad	Soup	Rice	Fried	Grilled

تُفّاح	بَطاطا	بَندورة	خَس	سُكَّر	فِلفِل	مِلح	فاتورة
Apple	Potatoes	Tomatoes	Lettuce	Sugar	Pepper	Salt	Bill

Conversation

The conversation below illustrates how to greet your server and order food at a restaurant.

مَرحَباً!
Hi!

أهلاً!
Hello!

هَل نَبدأ بالمَشروبات؟
Start you off with a drink?

نَعَم!
Yes, please!

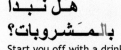

تَفَضَّلي!
Go ahead!

كأسٌ مِن الماءِ لَوسَمَحت!
A glass of water, please!

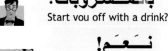

الوَجبات أو المُقَبِّلات؟
Appetizers or main course?

سَمَكٌ مَشوي وصَحنٌ مِن السَلَطةِ لَوسَمَحت؟
Grilled fish and a side of salad please!

مُرَطِّبات؟
Beverages?

ما هيَ أنواعُ المُرَطِّبات لَدَيكُم؟
What kind of beverages do you have?

مانجا، لَيمون، بُرتُقال، تُفّاح، فَراولَة.
Mango, lemon, orange, apple, strawberry.

مانجا لَو سَمَحت! شُكراً!
Mango, please! Thanks!

عَفواً!
You're welcome!

Dual System   المُثَنّى

Unlike English, Arabic utilizes the dual system of referring to two items. To form the dual of a noun, the suffix ان is added to the singular word. Example:

singular	Add suffix	dual
(house) بَيت	(dual marker) ان	(two houses) بَيتان

Practice

Change the following singular nouns into dual nouns based on the rule above.

	مَكروه Despised		سِياسي politician		مُطرِب Singer
	عازِف composer		لاعِب Player		مُحامي Lawyer
	مُمَثِّل actor		مَحبوب Popular		مُبَرمِج Programmer

Your turn to order

Take a classmate's order by writing what they request on the following sheet. Practice taking turns being the server and the customer. The menu contains some standard items available in restaurants across the world. Try and see if you can order some food for yourself. Practice with your classmate or your teacher

CCafe' we redefine food and beverage

فاتورة _____

الإسم _____

المَشروبات _____

المُقبّلات _____

الوجبات _____

Draw the customer
just for fun!

You can order by using any of the following expressions:

شاي لو سَمَحت (I'd like a cup of tea, please).

صَحنٌ مِنَ السَلَطة لو سَمَحت (A bowl of salad, please).

The teacher will check on students' orders by asking each person who they're serving and what that person ordered.

Did you know?

There are a lot of restaurants in the US that serve Middle Eastern food. Some of Middle Eastern popular foods are *hummus*, *falafel*, grape leaves, *shawerma*, and *tabooli*. Dearborn, MI, also known as Little Lebanon, is home to some of the best Middle Eastern restaurants in the US.

Blog

"This week we went over the restaurant vocabulary words. It was a good practice because I know them pretty well now. I've been trying to read words on my own, but it still takes a while to figure them out. I'm really nervous to record the conversation because I don't know if I'm saying the words right. They sound right to me. I think I remember all of them from class. It was good to go over them like we did; it helped me a lot. When we had to apply the words in the activity, I kind of had a little trouble because I wasn't sure if I was saying the words right. Overall, I am confident that I can read words; it just takes a while. Hopefully I'll get better with more practice." CD

Dictation

Write down the words that you hear from your teacher.

Connect the letters

Connecting the letters at this stage should become fairly easy. This is to cement your ability to connect the letters. If you're still having trouble, make sure you talk to your teacher or ask your classmates for assistance.

ك و ب	س م ح ت
ل ح م ة	م ع ل ش
دَ ج اج	صَ ح ن
خَ س	ك اس ة
س ك ر	ع ص ي ر
ه ش ، و ،	ش ، ر اب

م ق ل ي   ت ف اح

بُ رت ق ال   ب ط اط ا

ل ي م و ن   بَ ن دورة

The Definite Article أداة التَّعريف: ال

In Arabic, the majority of the letters are usually pronounced. Arabic has this rule that you pronounce what you write. Unlike English, where you may not pronounce the letters *gh* in the word *eight*, in Arabic, everything you write must be pronounced. However, there are exceptions. One of the exceptions to this rule is when the definite article ال is used. In terms of pronunciation, there are two types of ال: One where the ل is pronounced and the other type where the ل is not pronounced.

If the definite article ال is followed by any of the following letters, then the ل in ال is not pronounced.

ت ث د ذ ر ز س ش ص ض ط ظ ن

Otherwise, the ل is pronounced.

Example: In the following word, the highlighted letter حـ in الـحيـاة is not one of the above letters. Therefore, the ل is pronounced. To help you keep up with this rule in the book, instances of ال that are pronounced will be highlighted in green colors.

Silent or pronounced?

Decide whether ال in the following words is pronounced (p), or silent (s).

المَدرَسَة	البَيت	الفُقَراء	العُيون
المَسجِد	الشّارع	القَلب	المَلعَب
النِساء	الحَديقة	الدّواء	الكَراسي

The Present Tense: Third Person Pronoun

When the third person singular pronoun is the agent of a verb, a يـ (if masculine) or تـ (if feminine) is added to the beginning of the verb. Examine the first singular pronoun.

1   أنـا أعمَلُ في مِكدانـلز (I work at McDonalds)

2   هُوَ يَـعمَلُ في مِكدانـلز (He works at McDonalds)

3   هِيَ تَـعمَلُ في مِكدانـلز (She works at McDonalds)

Determining Prefixes and Suffixes

Determine the un-original letters in the following words (the letters that are not original in the root of each word)

مُذيع Broadcaster	مَكروه Despised	سِياسي politician	مُطرِب Singer
كَبير Old	عازِف composer	لاعِب Player	مُحامي Lawyer
صَغير young	مُمَثِّل actor	مَحبوب Popular	مُبَرمِج Programmer

Conjugate the Verb

Conjugate the verb based on the subject of each sentence in the following by adding تَــ or يَــ , أ

عـمَـل أحمَد في مَدرَسـة البَنين	ـ	تَ	يَ	أ	1
كـتُـب حنـان في جَريدة الأهرام	ـ	تَ	يَ	أ	2
سكُن أنا في كلارِيـن	ـ	تَ	يَ	أ	3
درس سمَيرة في جامِعة كامبرج	ـ	تَ	يَ	أ	4
سـمَع نادِر لِلموسيقى الكلاسيكية	ـ	تَ	يَ	أ	5

Pronunciation خ vs. غ

The pronunciation of the sound غ can be easily confused with the sound خ. To help you identify which one is being pronounced, your instructor will pronounce both of them in minimal pairs to help you identify which one is being used. Put a check mark next to the word you hear. You will be able to hear each example twice.

A	غ	خ	B
A	غَمزة	خَمسة	B
A	غَير	خَير	B
A	يَغبِط	يَخبِط	B
A	أغمَد	أخمَد	B

Verb Roots

Below are the verbs introduced in this unit. With the help of a classmate or your teacher, try to derive more words from the roots for each of the following verbs. TIP: A dictionary can tell you if your attempts are good!

Participle	Agent (doer)	Root
مَسموح permitted	سـامِح permitter	سـمَح To permit
		شَرِبَ
		كَتَبَ
		طـبَخَ
		خَلَط

Word Reference

This section lists all roots of the words introduced in this unit and their meaning. Make sure that you are familiar with the meaning of all these roots.

ء	ة	ي	ى	و	هـ	ن	م	ل	كـ	
		yes	when	hence	neck	met	lent	can		

العربية 30

Meaning	Root	Meaning	Root	Meaning	Root
To put out (put out)	خَمَدَ	To mix (mixed)	خَلَطَ	To hit (hit)	خَبَطَ
To make a loud noise (made a loud noise)	دَوي	To study (studied)	دَرَسَ	To be good	خَيَر
To permit (permitted)	سَمَحَ	To live (lived)	سَكَنَ	To prostrate	سَجَدَ
To cook (cooked)	طَبَخَ	To drink (drank)	شَرِبَ	To hear (heard)	سَمِعَ
To hide (hid)	غَمَدَ	To envy (envied)	غَبِطَ	To work (worked)	عَمِلَ
To write (wrote)	كَتَبَ	To fry (fried)	قَلَي	To wink (winked)	غَمَزَ

Spelling

Find the missing letters in the following words and correct them.

لَو سَمَحت اس عَ ير رَاب وب لَ ة ة دَجا

مَ وي مَق ي أرُ ش رِبة سَلَة رِبة ن لَ ن

تَ ـا بَ اط بذ ة س كَر فِل ج فا ة

Blog

"I'm still not doing that well with the hearing the spoken language and knowing what is being said, but I'm starting to get better. I still find writing it and the grammar to be the easiest part of it. For me, everything that we have learned about writing seems to stick a lot easier then speaking it." EJ

"What I found interesting is the amount of words that the English language borrows from the Arabic language. It is very hard but can become very easy as long as you actually take time to practice. I personally plan at least to take out 30 minutes of each day to help me on my journey of mastering the Arabic language. Also I feel as though personally I am getting better at learning the Arabic language. I also feel as though I can maybe order the correct meal in Arabic. Well at least hopefully I will without ordering the wrong thing. Another thing that I found was very interest in Arabic was how one word can mean many different ones. For example when you interpret you bet it actually is meant on my head in Arabic." TP

"The more information about Arabic that gets presented the more I enjoy this class. The assignments are challenging, but doable and easily presented in the textbook. The interactive format of the book makes it very easy to work with. The relaxed atmosphere of the classroom seems to be helping students get over the shyness that would otherwise make them hesitant to participate when the speaking part of the class comes up."JF

These are some of the words that English has borrowed from Arabic:, Algebra, Admiral, Algorithm, Alkalai , Almanac, Arsenal, Caliber, Candy, Chemistry, Cipher, Coffee, Cotton, Crimson, Gazelle, Giraff, Hashish, Henna, Jar, Jasmine, Lilac, Lime, Lemon, Loofah, Lute, Magazine, Mattress, Monsoon, Mummy, Muslin, Orange, Ream, Safari, Saffron, Scarlet, Sorbet, Soda, Sofa, (Wikipedia),

Writing الكِتَابة

In this lesson, we learned quite a bit about food, ordering, and food items. In this composition, you can write about your favorite food items, favorite restaurants, etc.

Hello! !مَرحَبا

Dictation

Write down the words that you hear from your teacher.

  6

  7

  8

  9

  10

Literary/Cultural Connection

صَحَتين و عَافية

This phrase is used when one comes across someone or a group of people who are eating, which means *Bon Appetite!* This expression can also be used when responding to someone when they offer their appreciation of food that you made or prepared for them.

Where in the World is this?

This is a shot of the Umayyad Mosque in Syria. (Image by Theklan)

مَتى المُباراة؟ What Time is the Game?

In this lesson, you will formulate questions to ask about the time, and say what you like to watch on TV at certain times during the day. You will also be introduced to prepositions in Arabic.

Did you know?

Soccer is the most popular sport in the Arab World. Many kids in the Arab world grew up playing soccer in the streets and alleys. Few Arab countries have qualified to play in the World Cup, for example, Saudi Arabia, Egypt, Morocco, Algeria, Iraq, and Kuwait. Qatar will automatically qualify since they are hosting the event in 2022.

المُفرَدات Vocabulary

مَتى	أيّ	تُريدُ	أشاهِد	بَرنامَج	المُباراة	ساعة
When	Which	Want	Watch	Program	The Game	Hour

فَريق	أحِبُّ	اليوم	لا مانِعَ لَدي
Team	I Like	Today	No Problem

هَل تُريدُ مُشاهَدَةَ المُباراةِ اليوم؟
Would you like to watch the game today?

أيُ مُباراة؟
What game?

الأهلي و النَّصر
Al-Ahli vs. Annusr

مَتى ؟
When?

الساعة السادِسة!
At six o'clock!

لا مانِعَ لَدي
Why not!

What's your favorite TV show?

To help you develop your listening skills, the teacher, or your classmate, will say what their favorite TV show is. Your job is to figure out what time that show is on. Shows' names and times are in Table 9. For extra practice, your teacher can bring a copy of a TV guide list of shows, and help students practice talking about their favorite shows.

مَتى يأتي برنامَجُ التَعليم في الوَطَن العَرَبي؟
What time is "Education in the Arab world" on?

السَّاعـةُ الـثّامِنـة و الـدَّقيقـة ثلاثون مَـسـاءً!

At 8:30 pm

نَوع البَرنامَج	الوَقت	إسم البَرنامَج
بَرامِج تَعليمية	مَسـاءً 8:30	الـتَـعليم في الوَطَن الـعَربي
بَرامِج وَثائِقية	مَسـاءً 10:20	دُروس مِن الحَرب العَالمية الأولى
رياضة	مَسـاءً 11:55	أخبار المَلاعِب
أخبار	صَـبـاحاً 8:00	حولَ العَالَم
دراما	مَسـاءً 11:30	الـحَسناء و الوَحش
العَاب	مَسـاءً 4:20	إربَح مَعنا
دراما	مَسـاءً 2:30	جُذور أصيلة

Verb Roots

Below are some of the verbs introduced in this unit. With the help of a classmate or your teacher, try to derive more words from the roots for each of the following verbs. TIP: A dictionary can give you the final word if your attempts are good! The changes are highlighted for you

Participle	Agent (doer)	root
مُبَرمَج programmed	مُبَرمِج programmer	بَرمَج To program
		خبَّرَ
		عـلَّم
		جـهَّز
		شجَّعَ
		سـمَّعَ

Dictation

Write down the words that you hear from your teacher.

Prepositions أحرُفُ الجـرِ

Prepositions in Arabic link words in a sentence together, and are also used with other words to indicate a reference to time, place, or reason. The most common used prepositions in Arabic are the ones below:

لِ	بـ	في	عَلى	عَنْ	إلى	مِنْ
for	with	in/at	on	About/via	to	from/of

Prepositions are followed by a noun, just like in the examples below:

يَذهَبُ شوقي إلى الحَضانةِ كُلَّ يَوم.

تَـبدأ مُباراةُ فريق فيلادِلفيا في مَساءٍ يَوم السَّبتِ.

يَـقرأ المُعَـلِّمُ كِتـاباً عَنِ التَـعليمِ العالي في الولايةِ.

Word Reference

This section lists all roots of the words introduced in this unit and their meaning. Make sure that you are familiar with the meaning of all these roots.

Meaning	Root	Meaning	Root	Meaning	Root
To arrive (arrived)	أتـي	To authenticate (authenticated)	أصِلَ	To program (programmed)	بَرمَج
To ready (readied)	جَهِـزَ	To love (loved)	حَبَّ	To launch a war (launched a war)	حرب
To become pleasant (became pleasant)	حَسُنَ	To lose (lost)	خَسِـر	To report (reported)	خَبِـرَ
To want (wanted)	رادَ	To win (won)	رَبِـحَ	To hear (heard)	سَمِـعَ
To root (rooted)	شَجع	To witness (witnessed)	شَهِـدَ	To Arabise (Arabised)	عَرَبَ
To learn (learned)	عَلِـمَ	To become knowledgeable (became knowledgeable)	عَلِـمَ	To divide (divided)	فَرَقَ
To prevent (prevented)	مَـنَعَ	To document/trust (documented/trusted)	وثِقَ	To become a citizen (became a citizen)	وطِن

Writing الكِتـابة

We learned about your favorite TV shows, sports, and things of that nature. Feel free to let your ideas flow in Arabic in the following composition.

Hello! مَـرحَـبـا!

Literary/Cultural Connection

This saying is often used in Arabic culture to emphasize the importance of a healthy active lifestyle. It translates to "A healthy mind is in a healthy body"

العَقـلُ السليمُ في الجِسمِ السليم

ق	ف	غ	ع	ظ	ط	ض	ص	ش	س	ز	ر	ذ	د	خ	ح	ج	ث	ت	ب	ا
fetch			thus				some	shark	see	zen	riot	the	damp			jig	thunder	taxi	bib	Adam

مَرحَباً عَزيزتي ! Hi Honey!

In this lesson, you will be introduced to a conversation between a couple in Arabic. You will also learn how to use the past tense. Verbs in the past tense are highlighted in the conversation.

Did you know?

Women have gained several rights similar to those gained by women in the US in the last 50 years or so. In several Arab countries, there are more women with college degrees than men, and women have also joined men in the workforce throughout the Middle East, particularly in the last 20 years.

Vocabulary المُفرَدات

المُدير	دون جَدوى	كُنتُ	لَكَن	كيفَ حالُكَ	مَع	حاوَلتُ
The Manager	Without Use	I Was	But	How Are You?	With	I Tried

		أنهَيتُ	مُتـَعَبة	مَوعِد	الدَّوام	عافاكِ
		I Finished	Tired	Date	Work	Bless You

Colloquial Arabic

You will learn how subtle variations in how certain words are pronounced can provide great deal of information about the speaker in a given situation. You'll also notice the use of words that have religious references. This highlights the influence of religion on how language is used. The way people speak in any language can give more information about not only what region they are from, but also, in certain occasions, their socio-economic background. The field of study for that kind of linguistic behavior is called sociolinguistics, the study of how people speak in different situations depending on who they are talking to, where, and the purpose of the conversation. Sometimes the differences are subtle, and sometimes they are obvious. The substitution of ء for ق for example is very common in Levantine Arabic (Arabic spoken in Jordan, Palestine, Syria, and Lebanon). Females in Jordan, for instance, tend to substitute the ء for ق more often than males.

مَرحَباً حَبيبـتي!
Hi Honey!

أهلاً حَبـيبي. كيفَ حالُكَ يا عزيزي؟
Hi Honey. How are you my love?

مِشتاقٌ لَكِ يا عزيزيـتي!
I miss you baby!

أينَ كُنتَ اليومَ السَّاعة السادِسة؟
So where were you today at six o'clock?

كُنتِ في مَوعِدٍ مَع المُدير. كيف كان يومُكَ؟
I had a meeting with the manager. Tell me, how was your day?

					ء	ي	ى	ة	و	هـ	ن	م	ل	كَ

can	lent	met	neck	hence	when	yes

36 العَربية

الحمدُ لله. عُدتُ مِن الدَّوام مُتَـعـبة.

It was alright. Finished work and came home tired!

عـافـاكِ اللـهُ!

God bless you!

و عافاكَ!

You too!

The Past Tense الماضي

Just like in English, the past tense in Arabic is used to refer to events that took place in the past. The past tense of any verb in Arabic is also the root of that verb, i.e., كَتَبَ. Unlike English however, a past tense verb is conjugated differently based on the subject of the sentence. In English, for example, no matter who or what the subject of the following sentence is, the past tense verb form stays the same:

-(He/they/the world/the dog) got mentioned.

In Arabic, certain pronouns require specific ways of conjugation as can be seen in Table 10

سَمِعَ	Verb conjugated	Pronoun	Meaning
	كَـتَـبَ	هُوَ	He
كَـتَـبَت	كَـتَـبَت	هِي	She
كَـتَـبتُ	كَـتَـبتُ	أنـا	I
كَـتَـبنـا	كَـتَـبنـا	نَـحنُ	We
كَـتَـبتَ	كَـتَـبتَ	أنـتَ	You (male)
كَـتَـبتِ	كَـتَـبتِ	أنـتِ	You (female)
كَـتَـبو	كَـتَـبو	هُم	They (male)
كَـتَـبنَ	كَـتَـبنَ	هُنَّ	They (female)
كَـتَـبا	كَـتَـبا	هُـما	They (two males/males)
كَـتَـبتـا	كَـتَـبتـا	أنـتُـما	You (two males/females)

Verb Roots

Below are some of the verbs introduced in this unit. With the help of a classmate or your teacher, try to derive more words from the roots for each of the following verbs. TIP: A dictionary can give you the final word if your attempts are good! One has already been done!

Participle	Agent (doer)	Root
مَـوعود promised	واعِد promisor	وَعَدَ To promise
		كَـتَبَ
		شَـرَحَ
		نَـقَلَ
		وَصَلَ
		بَـعثَ

Play Possum!

For this game, you need to come up with a "convincing" reason why you were late to your significant other's anniversary, birthday, big day, etc. You can ask your teacher to help you in coming up with an excuse. You will need to articulate in each scenario a sentence that describes why you did not show up, or were late. Some examples are provided below. Good luck!

Spelling

Find the spelling errors in the following words and correct them.

Pronunciation ط vs. ت

Arabic has sounds that native speakers of other languages may not be familiar with, like the pronunciation of the sound ط which can be easily confused with the sound ت. To help you identify which one is being pronounced, your instructor will pronounce both of them in minimal pairs to help you identify which one is being used. Put a check mark next to the word you hear.

A	ط	ت	B
A	طَرَقَ	تَرَكَ	B
A	طَبَعَ	تَبِعَ	B
A	أعطى	أعتى	B
A	بَط	بَت	B

Determining Prefixes and Suffixes

Circle non-root letters in the following words (the letters that are not original in the root of each word)

حاوَلْتُ	كُنْت	جَدوى	المُدير
عافاك	الدَّوام	مَوعِد	مُتـعَبة
أنهيتُ	وَعَدَ	كَتَبَ	شَرَحَ
نَقَلَ	وَصَلَ	بَعَثَ	تَرَكَ

طَبَعَ / تَبِعَ	أعطى / أعتى	بَط / بَت	بِساط / طَرَقَ

Word Reference

This section lists all roots of the words introduced in this unit and their meaning. Make sure that you are familiar with the meaning of all these roots.

Meaning	Root	Meaning	Root	Meaning	Root
Duck	(بَط)	To give (gave)	عَطِيَ	To make hard (hardened)	عتي
To tire (tired)	تَعِبَ	To leave (left)	تَرَكَ	To follow (followed)	تَبِعَ
To forward (forwarded)	حيل	To thank/to praise (thanked/praised)	حَمَدَ	To earn (earned)	جدا
To miss (missed)	شَوَقَ	To continue (continued)	دَوَمَ	To manage (managed)	ديرَ
To return (returned)	عَوَدَ	To knock (knocked)	طَرَقَ	To stamp (stamped)	طَبَعَ
To be (was)	كان	To forgive (forgave)	عَفَي	To appreciate/to endear(appreciated/endeared)	عَزَزَ
To finish (finished)	نَهَي	To adapt (adapted)	كَيف	To speak (spoke)	كَلِمَ
		To promise (promised)	وَعَدَ	To welcome (welcomed)	هَلَيَ

Writing الكِتَـابة

In this lesson, you learned how language is used in social functions like having a conversation with a significant other, or family member. Write a short composition about your family, friends, or significant other. You can introduce them here, or write something about them that you like.

Hello!   مَرحَبا!

Literary/Cultural Connection

بلادي و إن جارَت عَلَيَ عزيزةٌ وأهلي و إن ضَنّـو علي كِرامُ

Family is perhaps the most important aspect of an Arab person's life. Almost all activities in life revolve around family members, family matters, and an overall concern for the well-being of family members. Arabs care a great deal about their family, and Arabic literature has reflected that value in its description of familial relationships. The above line of poetry by Abu-Feras Alhamadani illustrates that significant relationship. It can be translated into:
"My country is dear to me even when it is unfair with me, and my folks are gracious even when they let me down"

في الـبـنـك At the Bank

In this lesson, you will learn how to use Arabic to open a bank account. You'll learn how to use the possessive pronoun (*his*), and you'll be introduced to numbers in Arabic.

Did you know?

The dollar is a used and accepted currency throughout the Arab World. If you happen to be in the Arab world, stop by any bank and exchange or dollars for a local currency to make purchases. Most banks in Arab world will be able to exchange your dollar money in local currency. Credit cards are not as widely used in the Arab world in general as they are in the United States.

Vocabulary الـمُـفـرَدات

هَوية	جاري	تَوفير	حِساب	أفتـح	أن	أريدُ
ID	Checking	Savings	Account	Open	To	I Want

بِ	مُمكِن	أساعدكَ	كيفَ حالُكِ	تودِع	مَعلومات
With	Is It Possible	Help You	How Are You?	Deposit	Information

Conversation

The conversation below illustrates how to open a bank account.

مَرحَباً
Hi!

أهلاً. كيـف مُـمكِن أن أساعدكَ؟
Hi! How can I help you?

أريدُ أن أفتَـح حِـساباً جارياً.
I'd like to open a checking

بكُل سُرور! أريدُ مِنك بِطاقة شَخصية وبعضَ المَعلومات.
Sure! I need an ID and some more information.

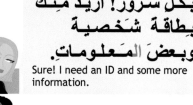

بالطبيع!
Sure!

هَل سَتودعُ شيئاً بالحِساب اليوم؟
Would you like to make a

ألفُ دينار
A thousand dinars!

تـفَضَّل الـوصل.
Here is your receipt!

شُـكراً
Thanks!

عَـفواً
You're welcome!

~				ء	ة	ى	ي	و	هـ	ن	م	ل	كـ
					yes	when	hence	neck	met	lent	can		

40 العَربية

Dictation

Write down the words that you hear from your teacher

Conjunctions: أَنْ

The conjunction أَنْ is used to form a clause after the main verb of the sentence, like a Catenative verb in English (*I hope to see my friend soon*), where أَنْ would be the equivalent of *to* in the previous sentence. أَنْ is followed by a verb in its base form, without any modifications, and the verb is in the accusative case.

أُحِبُّ أَنْ أَذهَبَ مَعَ أَخِي إلى الحَدِيقةِ

يُرِيدُ أَبِي أَنْ يَزورَ المَتحَف الوَطنِي في مَدِينة واشُنطُن.

تَعِدُ الحُكومةُ المُواطِنِين بأَنْ تَستَمِعَ إلى طَلباتِهِم.

تَتَمَنّى سُعادُ أَنْ تَسافِرَ إلى الصِين.

Possessive Pronouns

To create a possessive pronoun for the third person masculine pronoun (*his*), you add the following marker at the end of the word هُ .

Possessive Pronouns (his)

Complete the composition below using the information from the ID above.

إسـمُ مُقَـدِّمِ الطَـلَبِ   مِـهـنَـتُـهُ   و

39 سَـنَـة.   مِن نَـوع

رَقَـمُ   هُـوَ 9658458, و   هُـو البَـنـك

Identify the Numbers

Write down the words that correspond to the **bold** numbers in the following table.

11	14
9	8
2	3
10	7
5	1
6	9
4	12

Verb Roots

Below are the verbs introduced in this unit. With the help of a classmate or your teacher, try to derive more words from the roots for each of the following verbs. TIP: A dictionary can give you the final word if your attempts are good!

Participle	Agent (doer)	Root
مُوفَّر saved	مُوفِّر saver	وَفَّرَ To save
		حَاسَبَ
		فَضَّلَ
		أودَعَ
		سَاعَدَ

Spelling

Find the spelling errors in the following words and correct them.

Pronunciation ذ vs. ظ

In this installment of sounds that can be problematic, I introduce the letters ذ and ظ since they can be confused with one another. To help you identify each one of them, your instructor will pronounce both of them in minimal pairs. Put a check mark next to the word you hear.

A	ظ	ذ	B
A	ظَبِي	ذَكِي	B
A	ظافِر	ذاكِر	B
A	ظَرَف	ذرف	B
A	ظَنَ	ذن	B

Word Reference

This section lists all roots of the words introduced in this unit and their meaning. Make sure that you are familiar with the meaning of all these roots.

Meaning	Root	Word	Meaning	Root	Word	Meaning	Root	Word
To name	سَمي	إسـم	To help (helped)	سَعَدَ	أساعدكَ	To want (wanted)	رِيدَ	أريدُ
To prefer	فَضِلَ	تـفَضَّل	To deposit (deposited)	وَدِعَ	أودَع	To open (opened)	فَتَح	أفتـح
To run (running)	جَري	جاري	To become available	وَفِرَ	تَوفير	To deposit (deposited)	وَدِعَ	تودِع
To compute	حَسِبَ	حِساب	To compute	حَسِبَ	حاسَبَ	To run (running)	جَري	جارياً
To shed	ذَرَفَ	ذرف	To recall	ذَكَرَ	ذاكِر	To compute (computed)	حَسِبَ	الحِساب
To number	رَقِمَ	رَقَمُ	To please	سَرَّ	سُرور	To be smarter	ذكي	ذكي
To proceed	سارَ	السيارة	To thank	شَكَرَ	شُكراً	To help (helped)	سَعَدَ	ساعَدَ
To demand	طَلَبَ	الطَلَب	To forgive	عَفَوَ	عَفواً	To personify (personified)	شَخصَ	شَخصية
	ظَرَفَ	ظرف	To welcome	رَحِبَ	مَرحَباً	To be victorious	ظَفِرَ	ظافِر
To age	عَمُرَ	العُمر	Became possible	مَكِنَ	مُمكِن	To assume (assumed)	ظَنَنَ	ظَن
To learn	عَلِمَ	مَعلومات	To be of a kind	نَوع	نَوع	To prefer (preferred)	فَضِلَ	فَضَّل
To make a career in	مَهِنَ	المِهنة	To reach	وَصَلَ	الوصل	To become present	قَدِمَ	مُقَدِّم

Writing الكِتابة

In this lesson, you learned a bit about banking and opening a bank account. In this composition, you can write about your banking institution, your accounts, and some relevant information (Do **NOT** include actual banking information ☺

مَرحَبا!

Hello!

Literary/Cultural Connection

Parsimony is a trait Arabs despise. While being profligate is also a bad trait in Arab society, Arabs value generosity, and people who spend money to take care of others. The following line of poetry by Ibn Alroomi mocks a person who is very stingy. It translates to: "Isa is so cheap that he would only inhale from one nostril if he could, not realizing that he isn't immortal"

يقتّر عيسى على نفسه ِوليس بباقٍ ولا خالدٍ   ولو يستطيع لتقتيره ِتنفسَ من منخرٍ واحدِ

Meeting a Classmate التَّعَرُّف على زَميل

In this lesson, you will learn how to carry a conversation in Arabic between two people. They meet each other for the first time. This conversation takes place in a college setting. In this unit, you'll be introduced to cases in Arabic syntax, which allows you to be a better reader and better understand the grammatical system of Arabic.

Did you know?

Education is an important part of the lives of people in the Arab world. Elementary education is mandatory in most Arab countries till the age of 16. The ministry of Education in several Arab countries is the largest employer of any government agency. Because education is key to successful future careers, it is not uncommon to find people who sell their houses and property to be able to help their kids go to college. Most college students do not pay for their tuition. Usually, parents and/or guardians pay for their college tuition and expenses. While students in the Arab world try to work to help pay for some of college expenses, the kind of work available hardly pays for college expenses. Several universities around the Arab world provide scholarships to help students pay for their tuition. Some others, like in Egypt, for example, provide subsidized undergraduate education that can be afforded by the majority of students.

Vocabulary المُفرَدات

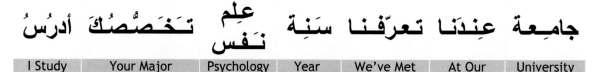

أدرُسُ	تَخَصُّصُكَ	عِلمُ نَفس	سَنِة	تعرّفنا	عِندَنا	جامِعة
I Study	Your Major	Psychology	Year	We've Met	At Our	University

		هُنا	بالتوفيقِ	حَضرَتُكَ		
		Here	With Best Luck	Your		

Conversation

The conversation below takes place between Michael and Ahmad.

ما تَعَرَّفنا على حَضرتُكَ؟

We have not met before. have we?

نادِية. وحَضَرتُكَ؟

Nadia, and you?

أهلاً نادِية. أنا فارس.

Hi Nadia! I'm Faris.

تَشَرَّفنا فارس. هَل أنتَ طالِبٌ هُنا؟

Nice to meet you Faris. Are you a student here?

نَعَم. أنا في السَّنة الأولى و أدرُسُ إقتِصاد. ما هُوَ تَخَصُّصُكِ؟

Yes, I'm a freshmen in Economics. What's your major?

أِ	ة	ء	ي	ى	و	هـ	ن	م	ل	كك	
			yes	when	hence	neck	met	lent	can		

44 العَربية

أنـا أدرُسُ عِلمَ النَّفسِ.

I'm studying psychology.

Role Play: What's your major?

In this exercise, you will engage in a similar conversation where you converse with a classmate regarding their major and what year of study they have completed.

الرِّياضِيَّات/ مُدَرِّسة	الأحياء/ عالِم أحياء	الكيمياء/ كيميائي	الصَّيدلَة/صَيدلي
الـتَّربية /مُرَّبي	إدارة الأعمال/مُديرة	المُحاماه/ مُحامي	الـتَّاريخ/ مُؤرِّخ
الرِّياضة/ رِياضي	الـفَّن/ فَنَّان	الـتَّصوير/مُصوِّر	عُلوم الحاسوب
الشُّرطَة/شُرطِية	الـتَّمريض/ مُمَرِّضة	الأدب الإنجليزي/أديب	عِلم النَّفس/ عالِم

مـاذا تَـدرُس / تَـدرُسين؟

What do you study?

أدرُسُ الـتَّمريضَ.

I study Nursing

To refer to someone's specialty or area of expertise, you can use this general phrase (مُـتَـخَـصِّـص في) that does not require any changing of inflections on the noun.

مُـتَـخَـصِّـص في الـرِّياضيات (specializing in Math)

Spelling

Find the spelling errors in the following words and correct them.

Cases: Nominative المَرفوع

The position of a word in a sentence in Arabic affects how it is pronounced. Depending on its position in the sentence, a noun may have one of several cases, a syntactic term that refers to how the word is classified in the sentence. Arabic utilizes three kinds of cases: Nominative, Accusative, and Genitive.

الكِتابُ ثَمينٌ . The book is expensive

You might wonder why the first noun الكِتابُ has an ُ at the end. This is due to its position in the sentence (being at the beginning). Because of that, it takes the nominative case. Most nouns that have the nominative case have an ُ at the end of the word. However, when the position of the word الكِتابُ changes in the sentence, or if it's preceded by other words, the case changes as in the example below

في الكِتابِ الثَّمينِ قِصَّةٌ

Note that the case of the word الكِتابُ changed from the nominative to the genitive الكِتابِ which is marked by the use of ِ at the end of the word.

Cases: Nominative

Provide the appropriate diacritics for the bold items.

فَريـق الجامِعة لِكرة الطائرة ضَعيفٌ.
شَعر حَبيبتي ناعِمٌ.
لَون سيّارتي أزرق.
عُمر أخي عِشرون عاماً.

Sentence Structure تَركيبُ الجُملةِ

Sentence types in Arabic can be divided in two main types: Verbal and nominal. In English, a complete sentence must have a verb. In Arabic, a sentence can stand on its own (have a complete thought) without having a verb. These are called nominal sentences. To determine if a sentence is verbal or nominal, one must look at the first element in the sentence. If the sentence starts with a noun, then it is a nominal sentence. If it starts with a verb, then it is a verbal sentence. A verbal sentence in Arabic usually consists of a verb, a subject, and an object and/or predicate. A nominal sentence usually consists of a noun and a predicate with some variations.

Verbal or Nominal

Decide whether the following sentences are verbal or nominal. Try to locate the verb if you can.

Hint

Nouns: Words that end in ــة are nouns. In addition, nouns usually follow prepositions (مِن —)
(إلى-عَن-على- في- بِـ)
Verbs: Words that start with a يـ or تـ and do not end with ة or ات can be verbs.

1   يَسكُنُ أحمدٌ في البيتِ _____
2   تَلعَب نادية في المُتَنزه _____

3 سَلامُ اللهِ عليكَ _____

4 في بَيتِنا رَجُلٌ _____

Verb Roots

Below are the verbs introduced in this unit. With the help of a classmate or your teacher, try to derive more words from the roots for each of the following verbs. TIP: A dictionary can give you the final word if your attempts are good! The first one has been done!

Participle	Agent (doer)	root
مُخَصِّص	مُخَصِّص	خَصَّصَ
		عرَّفَ
		فَضَّلَ
		دَرَّسَ
		علَّمَ

Pronunciation س vs. ص

The two sounds ص and س can be confused with one another. Listen to how your instructor will pronounce both of them in minimal pairs to help you identify which one is being used. Put a check mark next to the word you hear.

A	ص	س	B
A	صَبا	سَبا	B
A	صَومٍ	سَومٍ	B
A	مُصِّر	مُسِّر	B
A	صارَ	سارَ	B

How do you say it?

Below is the list of common jobs

بائِع   سائِق   مُعلِّم/ أستاذ   شُرطي   لحّام

جُندي   رَجُل إطفاء   قاضي   صَرّاف   أمين الصُندوق

مُربّي   ساعي البَريد   مُساعِد   طَبيب   مُحاسِب

You can ask your classmates about who they know occupies any of these professions as in the following example

مَن (تَعرف/تَعرفين) يَعمَلُ مُحامياً؟

Who do you know practices law?

جاك يَعمَلُ مُحامِياً

Jack practices law!

Word Reference

This section lists all roots of the words introduced in this unit and their meaning. Make sure that you are familiar with the meaning of all these roots.

Meaning	Word	Meaning	Word	Meaning	Word
Blue	أزرق	I study	أدرُسُ	Literature	الأدب
Treasurer	أمين	Business	الأعمال	Fire-fighting	إطفاء
Mail	البَريد	With good luck	بالتوفيق	Seller	بائع
We met	تَعرَّفنا	Your major	تَخَصُّصُكَ	History	التَّاريخ
University	الجامِعةِ	Expensive	ثَمينٌ	Play	تَلعَب
My beloved	حَبيبتي	Computer	الحاسوب	Solider	جُندي
Taught	دَرَّسَ	Specified	خَصَّصَ	Yours	حَضرَتُكَ
Walked	سارَ	Driver	سائِق	Athlete	رياضي
A greeting	سلامُ		سَبا	Courier	ساعي
Cop	شُرطي	My car	سَيَّارتي		سَوم
Youth	صَبا	Became	صارَ	Felt	شَعَر
Weak	ضَعيفٌ	Fasting	صَوم	Teller	صَرَّاف
Made knowledgeable	عَرَّفَ	Physician	طَبيب	Volley/flying	الطائرة
	عِندَنا	Age	عُمر	Science	علِم
Artist	فَنَّان	Preferred	فَضَّلَ	Team	فَريق
The book	الكِتابُ	Story	قِصَّة	Judge	قاضي
Accountant	مُحاسِب	Park	المُتَنَزه	Color	لَون
Educator	مَرَبِّي	Manager	مُدير	Defense	المُحاماه
Making happy	مُسِّر	Assistant	مُساعِد	Educator	مُرَبِّي
Nurse	مُمَرَّض	Photographer	مُصوِّر	Insisting	مُصِر
Live	يَسكُن	Psyche	نَفس	Soft	ناعِمٌ

الكِتابة Writing

So you learned a bit about words and structures used to describe majors of study! Now it's time to tell the world what you are studying, and why. Feel free to consult with a dictionary to help you use words in your composition.

مَرحَبا!

Hello!

Dictation

Write down the words that you hear from your teacher

Literary/Cultural Connection

Acquiring knowledge in Arabic culture has always been the foundation on which great things happen. Arabs value learning and literacy greatly, just like other cultures do. The following line of poetry reflects this value in Arab culture. It translates to: "Knowledge builds homes of endless foundations, and ignorance destroys the best of homes"

العِلمُ يَبني بيوتاً لا عِمادَ لَها   والجَهلُ يَهدِمُ بيتَ العِزِّ و الكَرَمِ

Where in the World is this?

Mecca is considered the birthplace of Islam. On Average, 2 million people make the annual pilgrimage to the old city from all parts of the world. The word *mecca* has been incorporated in the English dictionary, meaning a place where faithful people congregate. Mecca is a city in modern day Saudi Arabia. (Image by Meshal Obeidallah). Mecca is also known in the Arab and Islamic world as Makka Al-Mukarramah. مَكة المُـكـرَّمة

The image to the right is of جَبـل النّـور which is the place prophet Mohammed (PBUH) has received revelation from the angel Gabrielle. (Image by Adiput)

الشُرطةُ في خِدمةِ الشَّعبِ To Serve and Protect

In this lesson, you will be introduced to *Parsing* in Arabic syntax. You will be introduced to the concept of *Nominative Cases*, and *Idafa Constructions*.

Did you know?

Tourists in the Middle East are respected and treated very well. Several countries in the Middle East have police units dedicated to serving and protecting tourists during their visit to the country.

Vocabulary المُفرَدات

الصوص	تُحافِظُ	مُلابَسات	النِّظام	رجالُ الأمـن
Thieves	The Rule Of Law	Circumstances	Preserve	Police Officers

		الشُرطَة	الشَعبِ	تَحقيق	جَريمة
		Crime	Investigation	The People	Police

تَعمَلُ الشُرطةُ في خِدمةِ الشَعبِ ، حَيثُ تُحافِظُ عَلى النِّظامِ و تَحمي المُواطِنينَ. يُحاوِلُ رجالُ الأمـنِ البَحثَ عن الصوصِ و المُجرمينَ. عِنـدَ وقوعِ أيِّ جَريمةٍ ، يَبدأ رجالُ الأمنِ بِالتَحقيقِ لِمَعرفةِ الجاني و مُلابَساتِ الجَريمةِ. يَتَمتَعُ رجالُ الشُرطةِ عادَةً بِالإنضباطِ والسُمعَةِ الجيدةِ.

Reading Comprehension

Answer the following questions based on your understanding of the text above

مَن يَعملُ في خِدمةِ الشَّعبِ؟

ماذا يَفعَلُ رجالُ الشُرطة عِندَ وقوعِ أي جَريمة؟

بِماذا يَتَمتَعُ رجالُ الشُرطةِ؟

Parts of Speech

Determine the part of speech of the underlined words in the following paragraph (v: verb, n: noun, prep: preposition, adv.: adverb, adj: adjective).

تَعمَلُ الشُرطةُ في خِدمةِ الشَعبِ ، حَيثُ تُحافِظُ عَلى النِّظامِ و تَحمي المُواطِنينَ. يُحاوِلُ رجالُ الأمـنِ البَحثَ عن الصوصِ و المُجرمينَ. عِنـدَ وقوعِ أيِّ جَريمةٍ ، يَبدأ رجالُ الأمنِ بِالتَحقيقِ لِمَعرفةِ الجاني و مُلابَساتِ الجَريمةِ.

ء	ى	ي	و	هـ	ن	م	ل	كـ	
	yes	when	hence	neck	met	lent	can		

50 العربية

Spelling

Find the spelling errors in the following words and correct them based on the main text in this unit.

ظْ مُلابِ ات النَّ ام الذْ ص الشِّر الـ بِ

Verb Roots

Below are the verbs introduced in this unit. With the help of a classmate or your teacher, try to derive more words from the roots for each of the following verbs. TIP: A dictionary can give you the final word if your attempts are good!

Participle	Agent (doer)	Root
مَحفوظ	حَافِظ	حَفِظَ
		سَرَقَ
		خَدَمَ
		بَحَثَ
		بَدَأ

Cases: Genitive المَجرور

We talked previously about the cases and I mentioned that there are three kinds of cases in the Arabic language: Nominative, Accusative, and Genitive. I also explained that words with the nominative case have an ُ at the end of them marking their case. The second kind of case we'll discuss here is the genitive case. The genitive case is relatively simple. If a noun is preceded by a preposition, it takes the genitive case. The genitive case is marked by using the ِ at the end of the word. Consider the following example

البيتُ (Nominative Case)

في البيتِ (Genitive Case)

Notice that where the nominative case takes the ُ , the genitive takes the ِ . The preposition في changed the case of the noun البيت from nominative to genitive. Remember that the followings are the most popular prepositions:

مِن- إلى-عَن-على- في- بِـ

(Addition) Constructions الإضَافة

Consider the following example.

البَـيـتُ جَميلٌ .The house is beautiful

بَـيـتُ المُـدير جَـميلٌ . The principal's house is beautiful

In the above example, the head noun in the first sentence does not tell us much information about whose house it is. In the second sentence, however, we add another word to describe which house we are talking about (in the example, we added the word principal to describe which house is being discussed). The construction بَـيـتُ المُـدير is an example of an *Idafa* construction. As you can see, *Idafa* constructions are made up of two parts, the *head* noun (which always comes first) بيتُ and another modifying noun which is called the second term of Idafa. As far as diacritics and cases are concerned, there are two points to be noted. The head noun takes whatever case depending on its position in the sentence. The second term of Idafa is almost always in the genitive case.

يُحِبُ الأُسْتاذُ طُلاب الصَّف
Accusative head noun

يَتَحَدَثُ الأُسْتاذُ الى طُلّاب الصَّف
Genitive head noun

طُلّابُ الصَّف يَتَحَدَثون إلى الأُسْتاذِ .
Nominative head noun

As you can see from the above example, the head noun is affected by its position in the sentence, whereas the second term of Idafa is almost always in the genitive case.

Idafa Constructions

Rearrange the following words to make meaningful sentences.

الطّالِبِ / قَديمٌ / كِتابُ (1)
_____

إلى / يـعـودُ / الأُسـتـاذُ / المَدرَسـةِ / مَكتَـب (2)
_____

بـ/الجامِعَةِ / سِعرِ /تُباعُ / ثَمـيـنٍ/ كُـتُـبُ (3)
_____

يَقرأُ / العُلُـوم/ كُـتُـبَ / الطّبِّ / طـالِبُ (4)
_____

المَدرَسَةِ /الأطـفـالُ / يَـركَبُ / بـاصَ (5)
_____

Idafa Constructions

Provide the appropriate diacritics for the highlighted items

فَتـاة المَدينـة تَـعمَلُ في البنكِ (1)

أُسـتـاذ الجامِعَـة يُدَرِّسُ في الجـامِعَـةِ . (2)

يُـريـدُ الطّـالِبُ أفـضَل العـلاماتِ . (3)

شُـرطَـة القَريـة تَـخدُمُ الشَّـعبَ (4)

تَـذهَبُ الامُ إلى مَركَزَالتَـسـوق . (5)

يَـذهَبُ الابُ الى مَكـان العمـل . (6)

بيت الأمير واسعٌ (7)

فَتـاة القَريـة جميلةٌ . (8)

ساعـة الـذَّهَب ثَمـينةٌ . (9)

سَـيارة السِـباق سريعـةٌ . (10)

Solve the Crime

You're hired to help the police solve three crimes. You're given clues about each case, and your job is to help the police connect the dots and figure out what happened in each of these situations. These clues are not in any particular order. Good luck!

الكُـحول	قيـادة السيارة	حادِث

2 إفلاس	أشياء ثَمينة	السَّرقة
3 مُغازَلةِ/حُب	الثَروة/الغِنى	الموت/القتل

Word Reference

This section lists all roots of the words introduced in this unit and their meaning. Make sure that you are familiar with the meaning of all these roots.

Meaning	Word	Meaning	Word	Meaning	Word
Better	أفـضَل	Children	الأطـفالُ	The teacher	الأُسـتـاذ
Professional	الإنـضِـباط	The prince	الأمير	Safety	الأمـن
Started	بَدأ	The search	البَحثَ	Bus	باصَ
Investigation	تَحقيق	Preserves	تُحافِظُ	Sell	تُباعُ
Shopping	التَسوق	(you/she) goes	تَذهَبُ	Defend	تَحمي
University	الجامِعَة	Expensive	ثَمين	Make	تَعمَلُ
Better	الجيدةِ	Beautiful	جَميلٌ	Crime	جَريمة
Gold	الذَّهَب	Service	خِدمةِ	Preserve	حَفظ
Fast	سريعة	Stole	سَرَقَ	Race	السِباق
Car	سَيارة	Reputation	السُمعَةَ	Price	سِعر
Medicine	الطِبِّ	The student	الطالِبِ	People	الشَعبِ
Book	كتابُ	Old	قديم	Sciences	العُلوم
The manager	المُدير	School	المَدرَسةِ	Identifying	لِـمَعرفةِ
Office	مَكتَب	Center	مَركَز	City	المَدينـة
The system	النِظام	Success	نجاح	Citizens	المُواطِنين
Begin	يَبدأ	Occurrence	وقوع	Spacious	واسِعٌ
Ride	يَركَبُ	Attempts	يُحاولُ	Enjoys	يَتمتَعُ
Read	يَقرأ	Returns	يعودُ	Wants	يُريدُ

Writing الكِتـابة

So you learned a bit about words and structures used to describe majors of study! Now it's time to tell the world what you are studying, and why. Feel free to consult with a dictionary to help you use words in your composition.

Hello!   مَرحَبا!

Dictation

Write down the words that you hear from your teacher

Literary/Cultural Connection

Arabic poetry has long reflected Arab's beliefs on a variety of things in life, including life and death. This line validates that belief, that death is unavoidable, whether ones dies in a battle, or otherwise. This line can also emphasize the importance of not fearing death, an indication that one should be brave and willing to face this feat.

مَن لَم يَمُتِ بالسيفِ ماتَ بغيرهِ   تعددت الاسبابِ و المَوتُ واحِدُ

Where in the World is this?

Petra, a city carved in rock is located in the southern part of Jordan, in a town called Wadi Mousa وادي موسى. Petra, also known as the rose-red city, was built by the Arab Nabataeans in the 6th century BC. Petra has been designated as a UNESCO heritage site, and has been voted in 2007 as one of the world wonders.

تَعَرَّف على ساندرا Meet Sandra

In this lesson, you will learn how to form the possessive pronoun (*her*), form the agent and participle of tri-root words, and practice reading and conversation. This short essay is about the role of several international non-profit organizations that do a lot of good work in the Middle East.

Did you know?

The USAID, Fulbright, and the Peace Corps are some of the agencies that sponsor several development projects across the Middle East and the Arab world. These projects include building schools, the infrastructure, and the general economy. In addition, they dedicate several of their programs to youngsters and teenagers.

المُفرَدات Vocabulary

الشَّباب	أعمال	مؤلَّفات	صِياغَة	الولايات المُتَحِدة
The Youth	Works	Authored Works	Designing	The United States

تَهتَمّ	أمور	عُنوان	الطَّريق	السَّليم	التَوَصُّل	المُحاضَرات
Focuses	Issues	Title	Path	The Right	Reaching	Lectures

ساندرا هِيَ فَتـاةٌ مِن الـولاياتِ الـمُتَحِدة تَـهتَمُّ بِأمور الشَّـباب. مِن أهَمِّ أعمـالـها صِياغَـةُ بَرنـامَج رعـايةِ الشَّباب. مِن مُؤلَفاتِـها كِتـابٌ بِـعـنـوان " الشَّـبابُ أولاً". تُـرَكِّزُ سـانـدرا في الـمُحـاضَرَاتِ الَـتي تُـلقيها على أهَـميةِ الـحِـوار في التَّـوصُّلُ إلى الأسباب الـحَقيقةِ الَـتي تَجعلُ الشبابَ يَبتَـعِدوا عَن الطَريقِ السّليم.

Possessive pronouns (her)

To create a possessive pronoun for third person female pronoun (*her*), you add the following marker at the end of the word ـها .

Modified Noun in Sentence	Possessive Suffixed added to noun	Possessive Suffix	Noun
سَيَّارَتُها كَبيرة	سَيَّارتُها	ـها	سَيَّارَة
Her car is big	Her car	Her	Car

ء	ة	ى	ي	و	هـ	ن	م	ل	كـ	
		yes	when	hence	neck	met	lent	can		

العَربية 55

Possessive Pronouns (her)

Below is a report card for Lailah. Lailah is an athlete training for the Olympics. Ask questions about her by adding the possessive pronoun marker (هـا or ـها) and reading the questions out loud.

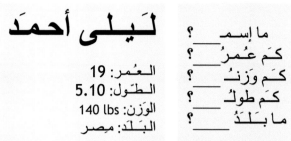

لَيلى أحمَد

الـعُـمر: 19
الطّـول: 5.10
الوَزن: 140 lbs
البَـلَد: مِصر

ما إسم ـ____ ؟
كَم عُمرُ ـ____ ؟
كَم وَزنُ ـ____ ؟
كَم طولُ ـ____ ؟
ما بَـلَدُ ـ____ ؟

Verb Roots

Below are the verbs introduced in this unit. With the help of a classmate or your teacher, try to derive more words from the roots for each of the following verbs. TIP: A dictionary can give you the final word if your attempts are good!

Participle	Agent (doer)	Root
مَرعي	راعي	رَعَى
		صاغَ
		إهتَمَّ
		أقـامَ
		أوصَلَ

Dictation

Write down the words that you hear from your teacher

6

7

8

9

10

Word Reference

This section lists all the words introduced in this unit and their meaning. Make sure that you are familiar with the meaning of all these roots.

Held	أقـامَ	Her works	أعمـالِها	Reasons	الأسبـاب
The most important	أهَمِّ	Took importance	إهتَمَّ	Issues	أمـور

First	أوَّلاً	Brought	أوصَلَ	Importance	أهَميةِ
Titled	بِعُنوان	Program	بَرنَامَج	With issues	بِأمور
Focuses	تُركِّزُ	Makes	تَجعَلُ	Country	بَلَدٍ
Reaching	التَوَصُل	Takes care of	تَهتَمّ	Which she lectures on	تُلقيها
Sponsoring	رعايةٍ	Dialogue	الحِوار	The truth	الحَقيقةِ
Sandra	ساندرا	Sandra	ساندرا	Sponsored	رَعَى
Configured	صاغَ	The youth	الشَّباب	Safe	السَّليم
Height	طولُ	The path	الطَريق	Configuration	صِياغة
On	عَن	Age	عُمرُ	On	على
Book	كِتابٌ	Girl	فَتَاة	Title	عُنوان
Lectures	المُحاضَرَاتِ	United	المُتَحِدة	Her authored works	مُؤلَّفَاتِها
Weight	وَزن	She	هِيَ	From	مِن
		To be further	يَبتَعِدوا	The states	الولايات

Civic Duty

Which one of the following volunteer or civic programs have you been part of you? Share your ideas with the class regarding when and where you participated.

المُشاركة في الإنتِخابات	التَعليم التَطوُعي	إزالة النِفايات	الحِفاظ على البيئة	مُساعَدة المَرضى
التَثقيف الصحِّي	البَحث عَن مَفقودين	الترحيل	مُساعَدة ذوي الإحتياجات الخاصَّة	رعاية الشَّباب

هَل سَبَقَ أن شاركتَ / شاركتِي في برامِج خِدمة المُجتَمع؟

Have you ever participated in community service programs?

نَعم. لَقَد شاركتُ في بَرنامَجِ مُساعَدةِ المَرضى في

_____

Yes, I participated in taking care of the elderly program at my community.

Writing الكِتـابَة

Have you ever done community work before? Have you ever been recognized for the work you do, whether formally or informally? Have you ever been part of something larger than you? If yes, you can write a small paragraph about an activity or event that helped shape your life or background. Feel free to borrow some of the ideas introduced in this lesson.

Hello!   !مَرحَبـا

Literary/Cultural Connection

The following line of poetry describes a general nostalgic mood Arabs have toward youth, and old age and wisdom. This line by Abu Al-Atahia translates to: "I wish I could be youthful again, so I can tell it what my old age has done"

فأخبِـرُهُ بِـمـا فَعـلَ المَشـيبُ   ألا لَـيتَ الشبـابَ يَعـودُ يومـاً

Where in the World is this?

This is the Dome of the Rock in the old city of Jerusalem. (Image by Wilson44691). This shrine was built by the Umayyad caliph Abd Al-Malik in the 7th century. Jerusalem is a diverse religious city, and home to the three monotheistic religions, Judaism, Christianity, and Islam.

Shopping التَـسَـوُّق

In this lesson, you will practice your conversation skills, form Wh-questions in Arabic, and practice your reading skills by being able to read and record the essay below.

Did you know?

Malls in the Middle East are not only shopping spots, but locations for people to meet each other and socialize.

المُـفْـرَدات Vocabulary

Buy	Market	Spend	The People	Things
يَشْتَري	السّوق	يُنْفِقُ	الشّعب	الأشياءِ

Kitchenware	Designing	Fruits	Food	Vegetables
أدواتُ المَطبَخِ	صِياغَة	الفَواكِه	الطّعام	الخَضْراوات

يَذهَبُ النّاسُ إلى السوقِ بِشَكلٍ إعتِيادِي، حَيثُ يَشتَرونَ العَديدَ مِن الأشياءِ الضروريةِ. يَشتَري النّاسُ مِنَ السوقِ الفَواكِه و الخَضْراوات ويَشتَري النّاسُ أيضاً أدوات المَطبَخِ، والملابِسَ. في الوَطنِ العَربيِّ، يُنفِقُ بَعضُ النّاسِ الكَثيرَ مِنَ النُّقودِ على الطّعام بِسَببِ كَثرَةِ الولائِم الَتي يُقيمونَها.

Understanding Comprehension Questions

To help you understand how to answer comprehension questions, examine the following components of the paragraph in this unit.

بِشَكلٍ إعتِيادِي   إلى السوقِ   النّاسُ   يَذهَبُ

كَيـفَ	أيـنَ	مَن
Adverb of Manner	Adverb of place	subject

الفَواكِه و الخَضراوات	مِنَ السوق	النّاسُ	يَـشتَري
مـاذا	أيـنَ	مَن	
Object	Adverb of Place	Subject	

بِـسَببِ كَثرةِ الولائمِ الّتي يُقيمونَها	عَلى الطّعامِ	الكَثيرَ مِنَ النُقودِ	بَعضُ النّاس	يُنفِقُ	في الوطنِ العَربيّ
لِمـاذا	عَلى مـاذا	مـاذا	مَن		أيـنَ
Reason	Object	Object	Subject		Adverb of Place

Reading Comprehension

Answer the following questions based on your understanding of the text above

هَل يُنفِقُ النّاسُ في الوطنِ العَربي الكَثيرَ مِنَ النُقودِ عَلى الطعامِ؟

ماذا يَـشتَري النّاسُ مِنَ السوقِ؟

لِماذا يُنفِقُ النّاسُ الكَثيرَ مِنَ النُقودِ عَلى الطّعامِ؟

Parts of Speech

Determine the part of speech of the underlined words in the paragraph below.

يَذهَبُ النّاسُ إلى السوقِ بِـشَكلٍ إعتِيادِي، حَيثُ يَشتَرونَ العَديدَ مِنَ الأشيـاءِ الضروريـةِ. يَـشتَري النّاسُ مِنَ السوقِ الفَواكِه و الخَضراوات ويَشتَري النّـاسُ أيـضاً أدوات المَطبَخِ، والملابـسَ. في الوطنِ العَربيّ، يُنفِقُ النّـاسُ الكَثيرَ مِنَ النُقودِ عَلى الطّـعام بِـسَببِ كَثرةِ الولائِم الّتي يُقيمونَها.

Possessive pronouns (our)

To create a possessive pronoun for first person pronoun (our), you add the following marker at the end of the word نا .

Modified Noun in Sentence	Possessive Suffixed added to noun	Possessive Suffix	Noun
جَامِعَتُنا مُمَّيزَة	جَامِعَتُنا	نا	جَامِعة
Our University is	Our University	Our	University

ك	ل	م	ن	هـ	و	ي	ى	ة	ء
can	lent	met	neck	hence	when	yes			

60 العَربية

unique

Possessive Pronouns (our)

Exercise: Modify the following nouns by adding the possessive pronoun marker نـا and reading the words out loud.

Spelling

Find the spelling errors in the following paragraph, underline them, and correct them.

يَـاذهبُ النَّـاسُ إلي السوقِ بِـشَكلٍ إعتِـيادي . يَاشتَري النَّـاسُ مِنـا السوقِ الفَـاواكِه و الخَـاضِراوات. في الوَطِنِي العَاربيِّ، يُـنـفِيقُ النَّـاسُو الكَـاثِيرَ مِنـا الـنُـقـودِي عَلي الطَّـعَامي بِـسَـابٍ كَثَرَتي الولائِم الـَاتِي يُـوقيمونَهَا.

Shopping List

Where do you buy the following items?

ادوات البِنـاء	ادوات الرِّياضة	الملابِس	المواد التموينية	الكترونيات
الأسلِحة	الهاتِف النَّقال	القرطاسية	الوَجبات السَّريعة	الأجهِزة الكهربائية
الأدوية	البرامج المرئية	الوَقود	مَفروشات	مُجَوهرات

مِـن أينَ تَـشتَـري/ تَـشتَـريـن الإلـكـترونيـات؟
Where do vou buv electronics?

أنـا أشتـري الإلـكـترونيـات مِـن بَـست بـاي
I buy electronics from Beest Bai

ء	ة	ى	ي	و	هـ	ن	م	ل	كـ
			yes	when	hence	neck	met	lent	can

61 العَربية

Shopping List

Get ready because you have some shopping to do! You need to fill out the list below of things that you want to get. Once your list is complete, you need to tell your classmates and your teacher about the things that you want to buy from the store!

أريدُ أن أشتَري دواءً مِن الصيدّليَةِ.

Word Reference

This section lists all roots of the words introduced in this unit and their meaning. Make sure that you are familiar with the meaning of all these roots.

Meaning	Word	Meaning	Word	Meaning	Word
drugs	الأدوية	Items	ادوات	Devices	الأجهِزة
usual	إعتِيادي	Things	الأشياءِ	Weapons	الأسلِحة
because	بِسَبَبِ	Visual	المرئية	Electronics	الإلكترونيات
grocery	التموينية	Construction	البِناء	In a way	بِشَكلٍ
Speedy/fast	السَّريعة	Athletics	الرِّياضة	Vegetables	الخَضراوات
food	الطَّعام	Necessary	الضروريـةِ	Market	السوق
abundance	كَثرةِ	The Arab	العَربيّ	Many	العَديدَ
Jewelry	المُجَوهرات	Stationary	القرطاسية	Fruits	الفَواكِه
Clothes	الملابِسَ	Electrical	الكهربائية	Many	الكَثيرَ
money	النُّقودِ	Furniture	المَفروشات	The kitchen	المَطبَخ
homeland	الوَطن	People	النَّاسُ	The items	المواد
goes	يَذهَبُ	Meals	الوَجبات	The phone	الهاتِف
Spends	يُنفِقُ	Banquets	الوَلائِم	Fuel	الوَقود
cellular	النَّقال	Put together	يُقيمونَها	They buy	يَشتَرونَ

الكِتَابة Writing

In this composition, you are to write about your favorite shopping place, or shopping event, shopping time, and other things that are related to shopping, buying, and selling. Feel free to write

about your most recent trip shopping, and feel free to let us know what you bought, and how much you spent (it does not have to be exact ☺). You could also write about who you would like to go shopping with, and why!

Dictation

Write down the words that you hear from your teacher

6		1
7		2
8		3
		4
10		5

Literary/Cultural Connection

This saying is very popular in Arabic culture. It emphasizes the importance of going to the market early to score the best deals. It is somehow similar to the English proverb: The early bird catches the worm!

مَن سَرا باعَ و اشتـرى

ف	غ	ع	ظ	ط	ض	ص	ش	س	ز	ر	ذ	د	خ	ح	ج	ث	ت	ب	ا
fetch		thus			some	shark	see	zen	riot	the	damp			jig	thunder	taxi	bib	Adam

In the City في المَدِينـة

In this unit, you will learn how to form the plural of nouns in Arabic. In addition, you will practice reading and recording a text about shopping.

Vocabulary المُفـرَدات

المدينةِ	أذهَبُ	مَعْرَض	العديد	المَحالُ	كَثيرة	كُلَ
The City	I Go	Store/Exhibit	Many	Stores	A Lot	All/Each

أذهَبُ إلى المدينةِ كُلَ أُسبوع.

يـوجَدُ في المدينةِ العديدُ مِنَ الأشيـاء، حَيْثُ هُنـاكَ المـحـالُ التـجاريـةُ، والأسواقُ. يوجَدُ أيـضاً الكـثيـرُ مِنَ السيارات. هُنـاكَ أيـضاً مَعْرضٌ لــلألعابِ فيـهِ أنواعٌ كَثيرةٌ مِـن الألـعـاب

Reading Comprehension

True or False: Decide based on the reading passage you read earlier whether the following sentences are true or false.

أذهَبُ إلى المدينـةِ كُلَ أُسـبوع. _____

لايـوجَدُ في المدينـةِ العديدُ مِنَ الأشياء. _____

يـوجَدُ في المدينةِ المَحـالُ التـجاريـةُ والأسواقُ. _____

Verb Roots

Below are the verbs introduced in this unit. With the help of a classmate or your teacher, try to derive more words from the roots for each of the following verbs. TIP: A dictionary can give you the final word if your attempts are good!

Participle	Agent (doer)	Root
		وَجَـدَ
		تـاجَرَ
		حَـلَّ
		أكـثَـرَ
		ساعَدَ
		عـرَضَ

~	ـُ ــٍ ــٌ	ء	ة	ى	ي	و	هـ	ن	م	ل	كـ
				yes	when	hence	neck	met	lent	can

64 العَربية

All/Each: كُل

كُل can be used in Arabic to mean *all* or *each*. When كُل is followed by a defined noun or an *Idafa construction*, it has the meaning of *all*; when it is followed by a singular undefined noun, it means *each*. Consider these examples:

All	Each
كُلُّ السائِقين في المَدينةِ يَجِبُ أن يَكونوا مُرَّخَصين	كُلُّ سائِقٍ في المَدينةِ يَجِبُ أن يَكونَ مُرَّخَصاً
All drivers in the city must be licensed	Each driver in the city must be licensed

Feminine Plurals جَمعُ المُؤنَثِ السالِمِ

In this section, you will be introduced to making plurals for feminine nouns. Later in this book, you will be introduced to masculine noun plural formations. Many of the feminine nouns (proper nouns that refer to females or nouns that end in (ة) are part of the regular feminine plural formation rule. To make plural of these words

1. Remove the ة from the end of the word
2. Add ات at the end of the word.

ساعة = ساعات

NOTE: Not all words that end in ة are subject to this plural rule!

Plurals

Change the following female nouns from singular into plural.

Plural	Singular	Plural	Singular
	مُساعَدة		مُعَلِّمة
	زِيادة		سَيّارَة
	جامِعة		مَكتَبة
	ناعِمة		بَطارية
	شَجَرة*		صَديقة

Writing الكِتابة

In this composition, you will be required to write about trips you make to the city, your favorite shops, stores, and things you like to buy from there. Feel free to include information about friends or family members you like to go with to the city.

Hello!   مَرحَباً!

Happy Eid عيدٌ سَعيد

In this unit, you will learn how to form plurals for masculine nouns. The reading text for this unit deals with the events people in the Arab world celebrate.

المُفرَدات Vocabulary

عيدٌ	يَحتَفِلُ	دينية	المُسلِمين	تَقاليدِ	وَطَنِية
Celebration	Celebrate	Religious	Muslims	Rituals/Traditions	National

عيدُ الميلادِ المَجيدِ	يَهود	المَسيحيين
Christmas	Jews	Christians

هُناكَ نَوعانِ مِنَ الأعيادِ في الوَطنِ العَرَبيّ: أعيادٌ دينيةٌ و أعيادٌ وَطَنِية. يَحتَفِلُ كُلٌّ مِنَ المُسلِمـين و المَسيحيين و اليَهود بأعيادِهِم حَسبَ تَقاليدِ دينِهِم. مِنَ الأعيادِ التي يَحتَفِلُ بِها المُسلمون عيدُ الأضحى و عيدُ الفِطر. يَحـتَفِـلُ المَسيحيين بِعيدِ الميلادِ المَجيدِ، و يَحـتَفِـلُ اليَهود بِعيدِ الفِصح اليَهودي .

Reading Comprehension

Answer the following questions based on the reading passage you read earlier.

هُناكَ نَوعان مِنَ الأعيادِ في الوَطنِ العَرَبيّ. إذكُرهُما .
هَل يَحتَفِلُ المسيحيين بعيدِ الفِطر؟
ماذا يُدعى سانتا كلوز في الوَطنِ العَرَبي؟

Cases: Mixed

In the following sentences decide whether the underlined items should be in the nominative case or the genitive case.

1. بَيتُ المُطربِ بونو كَبيرٌ جداً

2. مَوضوع الامتِحانِ صَعبٌ

3. علمِ بلدي جَميلٌ

4. حَربِ العِراق كَلَّفَت العَديدَ مِنَ الأرواح

5. حَصَلتُ عَلى العَديد مِنَ الجَوائِز في المُسابَقَـة التلفيزيونية

6. هُناكَ العَديدُ مِنَ العُروض المُغرية عَلى المَواقِع الالكترونية

7. مِنَ الصَّعب تَحديدُ مَن المَسؤول عَن التَحدّيات الَتي تُواجِهُ المُجتَمَع

Note: There are certain situations where the ِ is not used when a word has the genitive case.

Cases: Accusative المَنـصوب

The accusative case is perhaps the easiest of all. In a nutshell, objects in the sentence take the accusative case. Words with the accusative case are marked by a ً .

الـكِـتـابُ رائِعٌ
قَرَأتُ الكِـتابَ

The underlined item above is the direct object of the verb phrase ' I read' قَرَأتُ.

Accusative

In the following sentences decide whether the underlined items should be in the nominative case or the genitive case.

1. قَرَأ أحمدٌ كِتابا عَن صِناعَةِ السَّيارات
2. يُحاولُ رِجالُ الأمنِ البَحث عَن اللُّصوصِ و المُجرِمين
3. وَعَدَ أوباما الشَّعب الأمريكي بِمُكافَحَةِ الفَقرِ
4. تُحضِّرُ أمي طَبَقا مِنَ السَمَك كُلَّ يوم جُمُعَة
5. تُحاولُ شَرِكَةُ أبل لِلإلكترونيات السَّيطَرَة عَلى سوقِ الأجهِزةِ الخَلَوية
6. يَقرَأ مازِنٌ جَريدة الوَطَنِ بِتَمَعُنٍ

Plurals: Masculine Nouns جَمع المُذَكر السّالِـم

Many of the masculine nouns are part of the regular masculine plural formation rule. To make plural of these words

1. Add ون to the end of the word.

مُـعَـلِّـمٌ =مُـعَـلِّـمون

Plurals: Masculine

Change the following masculine nouns from singular into plural.

Plural	Singular	Plural	Singular	Plural	Noun

مُطرب	ليبي	أردُني
مُؤمِن	مُدقِّق	سوري
مُتَكَلِّم	مُساعِد	لُبنـاني
مُسلِم	مُبدِع	عِراقي
مَسيحي	مِصري	فلَسطيني
سَعودي	كويتي	بَحريني

Who's Celebrating?

Discuss who celebrates these festivals (Days) and when!

	كانون الأول December الثَّاني عَشر		
تِشرين الثَّاني November الحادي عَشر		كانون الثَّاني January الأول	
تِشرين الأول October العـاشِر مِئة		شبـاط February الثَّاني العِشرون	
أيلول September التـاسِع التِّسعون			آذار March الثَّالِث الثَّلاثون
آب August الثّامِن الثمـانون			نيسـان April الرّابِع الأربعون
تَموز July السَّابِع السَّبعون		أيار May الخامِس الخَمسون	
	حُزيران June السـادِس السِّتون		

ك	ل	م	ن	هـ	و	ة	ى	ي	ء	
can	lent	met	neck	hence	when	yes				

68 العَربية

The celebrations

عيدُ الأب	عيدُ الأم	عيدُ الفِصح	عيدُ المِيلادِ المَجيدِ	عيدُ الفِطر
عيدُ الحُبّ	عيدُ الفِصح	عيدُ الشُّكُر	عيدُ العُمَّال	عيدُ الإستِقلال

مَن يَحتَفِلُ بِـعيدِ الفِطرِ؟ و مَتى؟

Who celebrates Eid Al-Fitr? And when?

يَحتَفِلِ المُسلِمون بِـعيدِ الفِطرِ في نِهايةِ شَهرِ رَمَضان.

Muslims celebrate Eid Al-Fitr at the end of Ramadan!

Word Reference

This section lists all words introduced in this unit and their meaning. Try to restore the word to its original three-letter root (whenever possible)

Meaning	Root	Word	meaning	Root	Word
The units		الأجهِزةِ	Apple		أبل
Mentioned		إذكُرهُما	Ahmed		أحمَّدٌ
Spirits		الأرواح	Jordanian		أردُني
Al-adha		الأضحى	Independence		الإستِقلال
Electronics		الالكترونية	Celebrations/holidays		أعيادٌ
American		الأمريكي	The exam		الامتِحان
In		بِتَمَعُن	Security		الأمنِ
Their holidays		بأعيادِهِم	Obama		أوباما
Search		البَحث	Bono		بونو
Challenges		التَحدّيات	Bahraini		بَحريني
In fighting		بِمُكافَحَة	My country		بلدي
House		بيت	Rituals/customs		تَقاليد
Friday		جُمُعة	Attempt		تُحاوِلُ
Prepare		تُحضِّر	Specification		تَحديد

English	Arabic	English	Arabic
Televised	التلفزيونية	The love	الحُبّ
I had	حَصَلتُ	Face	تُواجِهُ
Newspaper	جَريدَة	Very/much	جداً
Beautiful	جَميلٌ	Men (of)	رجالُ
Fish	السَمَكِ	Prizes	الجَوائِزِ
According to	حَسَبَ	War	حَرب
Cellular	الخَلَوية	Cars	السَّيّاراتِ
The people	الشَّعب	Their religion	دينِهِم
Saudi	سَعودي	Santa	سانتا
Syrian	سوري	Manufacturing	صِناعَةِ
Iraqi	عِراقي	Market	سوق
Company	شَرِكَة	Control	السَّيطَرة
Thanks	الشُّكُر	Science	علم
Breakfast	الفِطر	Difficult	الصَّعب
Many	العديد	A plate	طَبَقا
The Arab	العَرَبيَ	Read (past tense)	قَرَأ
Kuwaiti	كُويتي	Bids	العروض
Easter	الفِصح	Laborers	العُمّال
Poverty	الفَقَر	For electronics	لِلإلكترونيات
Speaker	مُتَكَلِّم	Palestinian	فِلَسطيني
Book	كِتابا	Big	كَبيرٌ
Cost (past tense)	كَلَّفَت	Glorified	المَجيدِ
Person in charge	المَسؤول	Clause (Santa)	كلوز
Thieves	اللُصوص	Lebanese	لُبناني
Libyan	ليبي	Muslim	مُسلِم
Egyptian	مِصري	Believer	مُؤمِن
Programmer	مُبَرمِج	Creative	مُبدِع
Society	المُجتَمَع	Locations/places	المَواقِع
Birth	الميلادِ	Criminals	المُجرمين
Auditor	مُدقِّق	Glorified	المَجيدِ
Contest	المُسابَقَة	Promised	وَعَدَ
Is called	يُدعى	Assistant	مُساعِد
Christians	المَسيحيين	Muslims	المُسلمون
Singer	المُطرِب	Day	يوم
Birth	الميلادِ	Incentive	المُغرية
Celebrates	يَحتَفِلُ	Subject	مَوضوع
Two types	نَوعان	The nation/the homeland	الوطِن
Reads	يقرَأ	The Jewish	اليَهودي
		Tries	يُحاولُ

Writing الكِتابـة

Write about your favorite celebration, holiday, or any other event that has a very significant meaning to you.

Hello!   !مَرْحَبا

Dictation

Write down the words that you hear from your teacher

Literary/Cultural Connection

Celebration rituals in the Arab world vary from one place to another and from group to another. Yet, regardless of where you are in the Arab world, celebrations tend to be very festive events. People usually invite their families for food, visit each other, wear their nicest clothes, buy gifts to kids, and give charity to others on these days. These are fun events for almost everyone. Workers in general get at least two days off, while government officials tend to get a generous 5-day break from work. Schools, banks, and similar agencies are off for the duration of the celebration. A common phrase people say during these celebrations is

كُلُ عامٍ و أنتـُم بألِفِ خَير

This can be translated into: Seasons Greetings!

Elections الإنـتِـخـابـات

This unit features a short essay about elections in the Arab world. In this lesson, you will be introduced to the passive voice in Arabic and modifying clauses using الذي and الّتي.

المُفرَدات Vocabulary

النَّاخِبين	صَوتَ	مُرَّشَحين	صَنَاديقُ الإقتراع
Voters	Vote	Candidates	The Polls

يَتَنَافَسُ	الّلِجان	برامِجِهم	بإختيار	الأحزاب
Compete	Committees	Their Programs	By Choosing	Parties

تُعقَدُ الإنتِخاباتُ في مُـعظَم الدُول الـعربيةِ كُلَّ أربَـعةٍ أعوام، حَيثُ يقومُ الناخِبون بإختيار المُرشحين بَعدَ التَـعَرُّفِ على خُـطَـطِـهم ومُتـابَـعةِ برامِجِهم الإنتخابية. تُحدِّدُ مواعيدُ الإنتـخاباتِ وأماكنُ صناديقِ الإقتراع في مَوعدٍ مُسبقَ عن طريق الّلِجان الإنتخابيةِ. يَتَنَافَسُ المُرَشَّحون في جَمع أكبر عَددٍ مِنَ الأصواتِ بِوَضع اليافطاتِ والشِّعـاراتِ الـتي تَجذِب الناخبين. بالرُغم من وجودِ الأحزاب السياسية في العالِمِ العَربي، لايزالُ الإنتِخابُ يَتِمُّ على أسسٍ طائِـفية.

Who will you vote for?

Which of the following issues do you care most about? What common issues do you think voters all over the world care about? Express your opinions in this exercise where you tell the world what you care about in your world.

الطاقة	الأمور الإجتماعية	الجريمة	المُتَـقاعِدين العسكريين	البيئة

الفَساد	الفَضاء	الشؤون الخارجية	التَّعليم	الإقتصاد

ما هِيَ الأمورُ التَّي تؤثِر على إختيارك/ إختيارِك للمُرشَّحين في الإنتِخابات العامة؟

What issues influence your choice of candidates in the general elections?

التَّعليم و الإقتِصاد.

Education and the economy

Passive Voice المَبني لِلمَجهول

The passive voice is used in Arabic when the subject is not known or unimportant. The passive can be formed by changing the vowels and locations of these vowels into the form "yufaal". Passive voice in Arabic can't be used in the future tense.

Active Voice	Passive Voice
يَكتُبُ	يُكتَبُ
writes	is written
تَعقِدُ	تُعقَدُ
conducts	is conducted

Passive Voice Practice

Change the following sentences from the active voice into the passive voice. Make sure that subject of the sentence is removed when the sentence is changed into the active voice.

يَقرأ الأمريكيون جَريدةَ النيويورك تايمز كُلَّ نِهايةِ أسبوع .

_____

يُرسِلُ المُغتَربون المُساعداتِ إلى أهلِهم بِشَكلٍ دوري.

_____

Modifying clauses using الذي/ التي

الذي و التي can be used to describe/modify a noun using a verb phrase, i.e., The _student_ who is _eating right now in class will be asked to participate_. This sentence can be done in Arabic using الذي to modify the noun, _the student_.

سيقومُ الطالِبُ الذي يأكُل أثناء الحِصَّةِ بالإجابةِ بَعدَ قَليل.

تُقَدِّمُ الحُكومةُ اسعاراً تَفضيلية للسيارات التي تُوَفِّرُ الطَّاقة .

Practice الذي/ التي

Fill in the blanks with the appropriate choice of either الذي or التي in the following examples.

١ مِن أحدِ الأسبابِ ＿＿＿＿＿ تؤدي إلى مَرض السرطان هُو التَّدخين.

٢ تُوفِرُ الجامِعاتُ الظروف المناسِبة ＿＿＿＿＿ تُحَفِّز الطَّلَبة على الإبداع.

٣ الشَّخصُ ＿＿＿＿＿ يَقومُ بِمُعالَجَةِ المَرضى هُوَ الطَّبيب.

٤ زيدٌ هُوَ الطالِبُ ＿＿＿＿＿ قامَ بِتَعديل نِص مُحاضرةِ الأمس.

Dictation

Write down the words that you hear from your teacher

6

7

8

9

10

1

2

3

4

5

Writing الكِتابة

In this composition, you will be required to write about trips you make to the city, your favorite shops, stores, and things you like to buy from there. Feel free to include information about friends or family members you like to go with to the

Hello! مَرحَبا!

Literary/Cultural Connection

The main essay in this lesson mentioned that voting in Arab countries still in general takes place on a tribal or religious-basis. Separation of 'Church and State' in the Arab world is least evident. There are, of course, reasons for that. All Arab countries were colonies not too long ago (about 70 years ago) and as such, people were not allowed to participate in democratic elections. The tribe or larger family or even religious dogmas were a place of refuge and for support for people. Thus, a history of allegiance to the tribe and/or religious institutions that existed has continued to inform people's voting preferences. The events that have been taken place at the beginning of the 2011 year in the Arab world are a testimony that there is no country for old men, and that generations aspiring to freedom and democracy will write one of the most shining moments in recent Arab history. The struggle for freedom and free will has been a dominant theme in Arabic poetry. The line of poetry below by Abu Alqassim Ashabbi echoes that sentiment of the streets in Tunisia, Egypt, Libya, and Syria.

إذا الشَّعبُ يَوماً أرادَ الحَـياةَ   فلا بُدَّ أن يَستَجيبَ القَدَر
ولا بُدَّ لِلَّيلِ أن يَنجلي ولا بُدَّ للقيدِ أن يَنكَسِر

Short Essay: Life in the Village

تَتَمَيَّزُ العَديد مِن القُرى في العـالَمِ العـرَبي بِـالعَديدِ مِنَ الميزات التي حالَت دونَ زوالِهـا في ظلِّ نُزوح سُكانِـها المُستَمَر إلى المَدينة. أولُ هَذهِ الأسباب هُوَ التَرابُطُ الأسري الذي لَيسَ مَحدوداً عَـلى أفرادِ الأسرَةِ الواحِدة فَحسب، بَل على مُستَوى القَبيلةِ. ثانياً، يَعتَمِدُ أفرادُ القَريةِ على بَعضِهم البَعض في مُعظَمِ الشوؤن اليومية سواء كانَ ذلك الإعتِمادُ على الصناعاتِ اليَدَوية التي يُمارسُونَها أم على التَبادُل الزراعي و النَباتي و الحيواني مِمـا يَقوي الروابِط بَينَهُم. و مِنَ الأسبابِ الأخرى التي حالَت دونَ زوال القَرية طبيعتُها الجَميلَة حَيثُ الهواءُ النـقَيُ و الجِبالُ و الوديانُ.

Reading comprehension

Read the paragraph and try to answer the following questions

مـاهي الأسباب التي حالَت دون زوال القُرى في العـالَمِ العَربي؟

على مـاذا يَعتَمِد أفرادُ القَريةِ في شوؤنِهم اليَومِية؟

هُنـاكَ ثلاثَةُ أنواع من التَبادُل بين أفرادِ القَريةِ مذكورة في النص. عَدِّدها!

Notes

ق ف غ ع ظ ط ض ص ش س ز ر ذ د خ ح ج ث ت ب ا